From Fernando – Xmas '04

SPEAKING
OF
CHINESE

Raymond Chang

Margaret Scrogin Chang

SPEAKING OF CHINESE

W·W· Norton & Company
New York · London

To our parents:

Li Ju-fën (1901–1985)
Chang Jùn-shēng (1897–1966)

Hope Millar Scrogin
Frank Piety Scrogin

Copyright © 1978 by W. W. Norton & Company, Inc.

Printed in the United States of America.
All Rights Reserved

First published as a Norton paperback 1983; reissued in an updated edition 2001

Designer: Bernard Klein
Text type: Avanta
Display type: Codex

Library of Congress Cataloging in Publication Data
Chang, Raymond
    Speaking of Chinese.
Bibliography: p.
    1.   Chinese Language.   1.   Chang, Margaret
Scrogin, joint author.   II.   Title.
PL1071.C45   495.1   78-5553

ISBN 0-393-32187-8

W. W. Norton & Company, Inc.
500 Fifth Avenue, New York, N.Y. 10110
www.wwnorton.com

W. W. Norton & Company Ltd.
Castle House, 75/76 Wells Street, London WIT 3QT

2 3 4 5 6 7 8 9 0

CONTENTS

PREFACE

When *Speaking of Chinese* came out in 1978, China was slowly emerging from a long period of isolation that followed the establishment of the People's Republic of China in 1949 and the Cultural Revolution (1966–1976). Since then, Western contacts with China have increased enormously, as vast numbers of tourists and businessmen cross the Pacific. Yet on both sides of the Pacific, misconceptions abound. Many Americans still regard the Chinese as inscrutable, in part because of their language. We hope this revision in a new millennium will continue to enlighten people intrigued with the Chinese language on one hand and intimidated by its complexity on the other.

This book was first conceived as the result of introductory Chinese courses Raymond Chang taught at Williams College in the early nineteen seventies. In the years since our book was published, *Pīnyīn* (explained on page 33) has become the most common way to render China's official dialect in the Western alphabet. The Chinese capital, which the *New York Times* spelled *Peking* in 1978, has become *Beijing*. We expect *Pīnyīn* to be the standard spelling throughout the twenty-first century, so we have replaced most proper names and names of dynasties with their *Pīnyīn* equivalents, printed without accent marks indicating tone. Two familiar names from Chinese history, Confucius and Chiang Kai-shek, would be unrecognizable in *Pīnyīn*, so we have kept their traditional spelling. The beautiful Beijing dialect designated as the official language in both Taiwan and the People's Republic is called by different names in each of those places. We use its commonly accepted Western name, Mandarin, a word that has no Chinese equivalent. English speakers can generally sound out words spelled in *Pīnyīn* if they remember that *c* is pronounced *ts*, *q* is pronounced *ch*, *j* is pronounced *r*, and *x* is pronounced *sh*.

The widespread use of computers, with their alphabetic keyboards, has profoundly changed the way younger generations of Chinese students write their own language. These changes, outlined in Chapter Six, have resulted in a decline in the ancient art of calligraphy. Yet we believe that calligraphy is of such historical importance that we have kept our chapter on that subject intact.

We shall leave analysis of the social, cultural, political, and economic changes that have occurred in China over the past twenty-three years to scholars more knowledgeable than we are. Our attempt is to indicate the effects these changes have had upon the Chinese language.

We remain indebted to the Williams College Library and the Stanford University Library for making facilities so readily available when we wrote *Speaking of Chinese*. We greatly appreciate the kindness of museums, libraries, and individuals for granting us permission to reproduce art works and diagrams. Hope Scrogin helped with editing this book in its early stages. We thank Cornelius Kubler and Adam Wang for helpful discussions, Candace Watt, paperback editor at Norton, for her invaluable assistance, and Ed Barber, our editor, for his continued interest in our project.

Raymond Chang
Margaret Scrogin Chang
Williamstown, Massachusetts

SPEAKING
OF
CHINESE

One

SPEAKING
OF CHINESE

The language is at least three thousand years old. It belongs to the population of a vast country: to southern farmers growing rice in steaming paddies; to northern miners sleeping through winter nights on tile stoves; to nomads scattered across arid western plains. It is understood in San Francisco and São Paulo, London and Singapore. It unites more human beings than any other language of mankind.

Most people who do not speak the language think it extraordinarily difficult. Yet it is without regular or irregular verb conjugation, gender, or plurals. No spelling rules apply.

The best tool for writing the language is a brush, and

the person wielding the brush creates an individual work of art with every letter or grocery list he writes. To discerning readers, his handwriting is as important as his message. The artist paints his pictures with a writing brush, creating images with the same technique he uses to set down words.

Throughout their long history, people united by the language nurtured a reverence for the written word that no other culture has yet surpassed. They incised it into the plastrons of turtles and the shoulder blades of oxen, inscribed it on bronze, iron, pottery, stone, jade, and ivory, painted it on porcelain, wrote it on strips of bamboo, lengths of silk, and sheets of the world's first paper.

The language is Chinese.

Our book serves as an introduction to Chinese for the general reader. We speak to city dwellers intrigued with calligraphy sizzling from Chinatown signboards, to devotees of Chinese food, and to people who have always been drawn by things Chinese. Tourists or businessmen heading for China may find our book useful, as will beginning students of Chinese culture. Our book is for anyone who wants to know more about Chinese without learning to speak or write it.

We will not try to teach Chinese in "Six Easy Lessons." Spoken Chinese is best learned from native speakers, on tape or in person, while mastery of the written form takes at least a year of daily practice. We have tried to design a book you can read in bed without a pencil. We hope it will whet your interest in the Chinese language.

Scholars tell us that Chinese should properly be named

"Sinitic." The Chinese call themselves and their language "Han," recalling the glorious Han dynasty (202 B.C.–220 A.D.) that ruled China while the Roman Empire flourished.* Chinese is one of the Sino-Tibetan languages along with Tibetan and Burmese. The group has connections with Thai, the language of Thailand, and some linguists even relate it to language groups of the South Pacific.

A knowledge of Chinese has for centuries been essential to scholars all over Asia, as Latin was to scholars and diplomats of Renaissance Europe. In the third century A.D., the Japanese appropriated Chinese characters to write their spoken language, which has no linguistic ties to Chinese. Koreans and Vietnamese borrow heavily from Chinese, especially for literary writing.

Not everyone in China speaks Chinese the same way. There are many dialects deviating from the standard Mandarin of Peking, the capital of China for nearly eight hundred years. These dialects can be as different as English, German, Dutch, and Danish, but they share a common written language, understood by literate Chinese regardless of dialect.

This situation has some interesting consequences.

Movie companies in Hong Kong hire the best Mandarin speakers they can find for their action-filled epics produced weekly for worldwide distribution. Mandarin is the official language of Taiwan, where Hong Kong movies

---

*There is a list of the major Chinese dynasties and an East-West Timeline in Appendix 1.

are shown to avid fans, as well as of the Chinese Mainland, where Hong Kong movies are selectively distributed. To the rest of the Cantonese-speaking movie audiences throughout Southeast Asia and North America, Mandarin is almost like a foreign language.

In this country, Americans entering a movie house in any Chinatown might wonder at sometimes seeing sub-

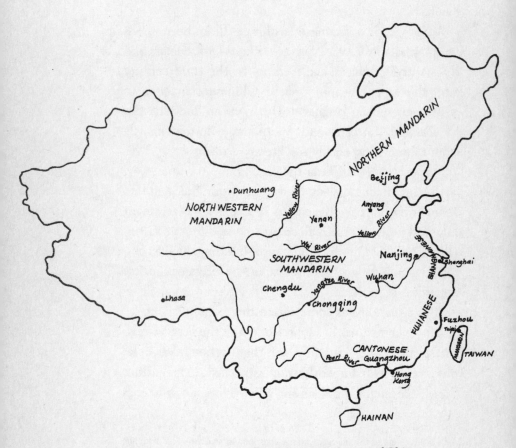

Fig. 1.1. Linguistic map of China.

titles written in Chinese for a Chinese movie aimed at Chinese viewers. They are thoughtfully provided by movie companies so their Cantonese audience can read what the Mandarin-speaking actors are saying.

Figure 1.1 shows the major dialects of China.* There may be dozens of subdialects within each broad area, some close to the main dialect, some quite different. A Beijing native venturing to tour the eastern half of his country, where 95 percent of all Chinese live, follows the Yellow River west along its course through the once luxuriant plain that four thousand years ago nourished an embryonic Chinese civilization. Although the spoken language changes subtly with every passing kilometer, it is still familiar as he leaves the sophisticated environs of Beijing and travels up toward mountainous country covered with loess, a windblown yellow soil.

All about him are the signs of China's struggle — successful at this moment in history — with the Yellow River, at once the source of water and life for a densely populated region and "China's Sorrow" when its sudden, violent floods are followed by drought, famine, and disease. Little rice grows here: the northern Chinese cultivate wheat as a basic grain, and when there is enough of it the people grow taller than southern Chinese, who eat less nutritive rice. Crossing the Great Wall to follow the Yellow River as it curves north around the Ordos Desert,

---

*We have used commonly accepted Western spellings for most proper names. Otherwise, we spell Chinese words according to Pīnyīn Romanization. The problems of writing Chinese in the Roman letters used for Western languages will be discussed in Chapter 2.

where population is sparse and verbal communication infrequent, the traveler enters a region inhabited by non-Han Mongolians, nourished on hearty soups they cook in coal-filled "hot pots." The Mongolian language, both written and spoken, is totally foreign to Chinese, but our tourist from Beijing, enveloped in a down-filled silk jacket and shouting against winds natives from North Dakota or Montana would recognize as their own, can still communicate with the Han Chinese he encounters.

Fig. 1.2. Hot pot.

Touring south, the wayfarer uses a rapidly improving road and rail system to make his way across the continuous east-west mountain ranges barricading the province of Sichuan, an agricultural paradise sometimes called the "Middle West" of China, where crops grow as high as the corn and wheat in the fields of Indiana and Iowa. When spicy Szechwanese food sets fire to his palate, the waiter understands his request for tea, but identifies him immediately as a Beijing native by his accent, conspicuous among speakers of Southwestern Mandarin.

Wending east again along the legendary gorges of the Yangtze River, our traveler views landscapes made famous by fifteen generations of painters and hears a language sounding less familiar as he goes. Shanghai, where the Yangtze flows to the sea, is China's largest city. Once it was a cosmopolitan seaport, with whole sections reserved for the exclusive use of foreigners. The man from Beijing visits a park in the old British concession to see for himself the famous sign, still preserved, that says "No Dogs or Chinese Allowed." His taste buds find relief from Sichuanese peppers in Shanghainese noodles and hot pastries, but, except for a word or two, he can barely understand Shanghai speech.

Relieved as a San Franciscan leaving Los Angeles, the tourist departs from Shanghai to go down along the coast through Fujian, the province of butchers and barbers, whose emigrants can speak their secrets safely among other Chinese, because few outsiders understand their language. Detouring inland to observe fields of tea and hear Kejia, yet another dialect he cannot understand, he finds himself at last in southern China, where a native of Florida or Louisiana would feel at home in the warm, rainy climate. Here, if the rains come at the right time, the land is fertile enough to support two rice crops a year, grown on terraced paddies. In spite of this abundance, South China has never produced enough food for the small, volatile people populating its cities and hamlets. This region breeds revolutionaries; occasionally a southern firebrand like Sun Yat-sen has changed the course of Chinese history.

Arriving in Guangzhou, the capital of Guangdong Province, our Beijing traveler finds the signs and newspapers familiar but the spoken language totally incomprehensible. Even some characters change their meaning

水
shuǐ
(water)

according to local slang. An example is the word for *water*. In addition to its normal meaning, the Cantonese also use it to mean *money* in slang.

Cantonese speakers are at an even greater disadvantage than the Mandarin speaker roaming in their midst, for the official spoken language of their own government is foreign to them. Most Americans have less trouble learning Mandarin than do Cantonese. There is a Chinese saying which goes, "We do not fear the sky or the earth. What we fear is hearing a Cantonese speak Mandarin."

Most of the emigrants from China during the century between 1840 and 1940 were Cantonese, perhaps because of this kind of snobbery, certainly because of the poverty of South China. The mountains of Guangdong Province have always prevented easy communication, so Cantonese is fragmented into a great many subdialects which emigrants carried all over the world. Even today, the Chinese you hear on the streets of San Francisco's Chinatown will probably not be Mandarin, but the particular dialect of a remote village in Guangdong.

Contemporary Chinese families, dislocated by years of civil strife, might share several dialects. A family at home in Shanghai before the Second World War might consist of a father from Fujian Province, speaking Fujianese, a mother from Sichuan, speaking a subdialect of Southwestern Mandarin, and children who know their parents' dialects but are also learning Shanghainese on the streets and standard Mandarin in school. After the war, the whole family may have moved to Hong Kong, where they had to become accustomed to such strange new foods as

wonton and egg fu yung, and assimilate a new language
—Cantonese.

The youngsters of this family can be compared to the
child of an American mother and an Austrian father in
Zurich who speaks the local dialect of German with his
early playmates and in primary school, pure German in
lycée or high school, English or Low German to his
grandparents, and French when he travels to Geneva.
There is, however, an important difference. Each language the Swiss child understands is expressed by a phonetic alphabet he must learn to write as he learns to speak,
while all the dialects of Chinese for the past three thousand years have been expressed in a single written language, a living language which has grown and changed
but not branched far from its original course.

Geographically isolated from other cultures through
much of its history and developing early a higher degree
of civilization than any of its nearest neighbors, China
generally dealt with foreigners as uncouth barbarians.
Until the nineteenth century, only one major foreign
influence had a broad impact on China: Buddhism from
India. The Chinese language has developed in a geo-
graphical vacuum, apart from outside influence. To
Americans, whose language is a hodgepodge of Anglo-
Saxon, Norman French, Latin, and Greek, who cannot
read what their direct ancestors wrote as recently as seven
hundred years ago, this unbroken flow of language
through the millennia should be a cause of wonder and
fascination.

Two

WRITTEN CHINESE

Phoenician

Greek

Roman

Ever since those seafaring businessmen, the Phoenicians, taught their method of writing to customers around the Mediterranean, Western man has used a small collection of symbols to represent the sounds of his speech. The Greeks traded with the Phoenicians, adopted their phonetic alphabet, then used it to write down the poetry attributed to Homer. The Romans took this alphabet from the Greeks and spread it all over Europe. Written words followed changes in spoken language as new tongues branched out and old ones withered away.

Before the Phoenicians spread their alphabet, writing around the Mediterranean had been ideographic, with highly simplified pictures used to represent ideas. All

12

written languages started out as ideographic, including Chinese, but China never did replace pictures of ideas with symbols for sounds. Instead, primitive picture writing was refined into an intricate, highly sophisticated system of ideograms.

The enormous difference between these two kinds of writing is often hard for Westerners, in whom a phonetic alphabet is ingrained, to grasp. In the West, the word we call ourselves, in English *man*, in French *homme*, in Spanish *hombre*, in German *Mensch*, is spelled with letters showing its pronunciation in each language. The Chinese express the idea by drawing a man walking on two legs. In Beijing, people would say this word as *rén*, in Canton as *yan*, in Shanghai as *nin*, in Japan as *hitoh*, in Korea as *in*. Two millennia ago, Confucius would have pronounced 人 differently. Yet all over Asia and across two thousand years of time, people who cannot comprehend each other's speech read this character and understand its meaning.

An ideographic written language has disadvantages, the most obvious being the number of ideograms a person must learn to read. Remember, we are not dealing with twenty-six symbols combined in various ways to form thousands of words. We are dealing with a *different symbol* for each of those thousands of words. A Chinese child must study much longer than an American child just to learn the rudiments of his own language. Dictionaries and telephone books are clumsy servants in China.

Even so, the virtues of Chinese ideograms entice the most pragmatic of minds. No one can underestimate their value as bonds between people separated by vast distances of time and space. In ancient times, Chinese was the language of scholars from Tibet to Kyoto. Today, a newspaper published in Beijing or Taipei can be read all over the world by people who have never visited those cities and could not communicate in speech if they did. While spoken Chinese has changed over the years just as all languages have, Chinese characters have not changed, because they are not phonetic.

As pictures of ideas, Chinese characters reveal the human mind at work. They travel directly from eye to brain, bypassing pathways of speech. Westerners who never quite master spelling, whose deepest responses are to pictures, will find themselves drawn to written Chinese. Its appeal to the artistic eye is unequaled by the Western alphabet.

A page of Chinese writing is traditionally read from right to left, up and down in columns.* Chinese books and magazines usually open from left to right, the reverse of Western practice. At a newsstand in Chinatown, flip through a Hong Kong movie magazine. Opened like an American journal, it offers an advertisement for a huge wristwatch on the "front" cover, and obscure news and lists of pen pals on the "first" page. Turn the magazine so the spine is in your right hand, and the fresh face of a starlet cover girl smiles up at you. Just inside what should be the back cover are lead stories on the romances

---

*Today on the Chinese Mainland, newspapers and magazines are often printed Western style in horizontal lines.

of Hong Kong's movie kings and queens.

About 25,000 Chinese characters exist; most of them fall in one of five groups. The smallest group, and the simplest, contains characters descended directly from ancient picture writing, like the ones shown in Table 2.1.

Table 2.1. Pictographs

Ancient form	Modern form	Pronounced	English
⊙	日	rì	sun or day*
☽	月	yuè	moon or month
🏺	酒	jiŭ	wine
⋀	山	shān	mountain
⊞	田	tián	field
▽	口	kŏu	mouth
川	水	shuĭ	water
川	川	chuān	river
𡚽	女	nŭ	woman
屮	手	shŏu	hand
⊘	回	huí	return to

*Proving that the Chinese were the first to discover sunspots.

The words for *sun* and *moon* clearly reveal their pictographic origins, and the modern character for *wine* still resembles a jug. The three small lines at the left of the wine jug are part of all words connected with water. (More on them later.) Mountains never change, though the character for *mountain* is considerably altered by the wear of years. The fields below the mountains are still divided into four parts for plowing as they were thousands of years ago.

Pictures are fine for describing concrete objects, but what about concepts like *up, down, small,* or *large?* Another kind of character is the *ideograph,* a drawing or symbol representing an abstract idea. Table 2.2 lists a few ideographic characters used to express position, size, number, and shape.

Table 2.2. Ideographs

Character	Pronounced	English
上	shàng	up
下	xià	down
中	zhōng	middle
大	dà	large
小	xiǎo	small
一	yī	one
二	èr	two
三	sàn	three
凹	āo	concave
凸	tū	convex

Ideographic characters are such ingenious pictures of ideas that they hardly need translation, let alone explanation. Only the words *large* and *small* do not immediately reveal their origin as sketches of a man flinging his arms wide in an expansive gesture, then bringing his fingers close together, defining a tiny space. We should say a few words here about Chinese numbers; there will be more to say when we reach Chapter 6. Being a practical people, the Chinese do not carry the system of lines past *three;* *four* is not 三 ! Otherwise, a number as small as *fifteen* would take some time to read.

Now things begin to get more involved. Words can be combined to create "hybrids," a third group of Chinese characters symbolizing increasingly complex ideas. Word associations developed over the centuries are witty and often deeply philosophical. In fact, hybrids may be the most fascinating of all five groups, for the trained eye can follow the logic of association and guess the approximate meaning. Chinese using these characters daily seldom think of the separate parts, any more than English-speaking people think of *cutlet* as a little cut, *cupboard* as a board for cups, or *breakfast* as breaking the long night's fast. Because the untrained eye may find these characters enigmatic, however intriguing, we will explain a few interesting hybrids.

When the pictographs for *sun* and *moon,* illustrated earlier, are placed side by side, the new character means *bright.*

明
míng
(bright)

The character meaning *force* or *muscle work* is 力 . When this character is placed below the character for *field,* another pictograph we saw before, the hybrid character represents *male.*

力
lí
(force)

男
nán
(male)

Now, if 力 is combined with 少 , *small* or *scarce,* the new character means *poor* or *bad.*

少
shǎo
(small)

岁
liè
(poor)

The Chinese write *eye* as 目 and *hand* as 手 . Shading the eyes with one hand is a traditional pantomime for

手
shǒu
(hand)

目
mù
(eye)

亡
máng
(die)

看
kàn
(look)

盲 人
máng rén
(blind man)

仙
xiān
(fairy)

信
xin
(trust)

言
yán
(speech)

舌
shé
(tongue)

話
huà
(speech)

拜
bài
(salute)

look, and so it is that the character *to see* or *to look at* shows hand above eye.

At the left we see the word for *blind man*. The first character places 亡 , *die* or *dead*, above the character for *eye*, forming the word *blind*.

Chinese oral tradition is full of fairy tales, many based on Taoist mythology. The word for *fairy*, written in the margin, contains two characters we have met before. The left part, 亻, is a variant of 人, *man*, always used in combination with other characters. The right part is the pictograph for *mountain*. While Chinese fairies live mostly in the Daoist heaven, sometimes they come down to the high mountains of earth.

The word *speech* is written 言 . Combining this character with the variant form of *man* creates the word *trust*. (This hybrid also means *letter* or *correspondence*.) In China, your trust of a man is founded on what he says. Another hybrid word using the character for *speech* shows that Chinese can be redundant as well as wise. Take the word *speech*, add the word *tongue*, and what do you have? Another character meaning *speech*.

We have already seen the character for *hand*, 手 When the Chinese want to congratulate someone or pay respects, they place two hands together, and when they write *salute* or *worship*, they place two *hand* characters side by side. Note that an extra stroke is added to the *hand* character on the right.

The ways of writing *marry* underscore the male dominance of old Chinese society. There are two different ideograms for the word *marry*. When a man marries, the

Chinese write a character with 取 , or *take,* above, and a 女 , or *female,* below. This combination means literally *take a woman.* Now, when a woman marries, the Chinese write the *female* symbol to the left of a character meaning *home* or *family.* A Chinese woman submissively joined her husband's family—often leaving her own forever—while a Chinese man forcefully took a wife. These characters are no longer used on the Mainland, for they are one small link in the ancient shackles broken by the Communists as part of a sweeping campaign to emancipate Chinese women. Instead, the compound word *jiē hūn,* meaning *to get married,* is used. The character on the right of *hūn* is a phonetic indicator which is also pronounced *hūn.* When it is written alone, 昏 means *dark* or *confused.* There's a warning for any starry-eyed young lover!

取
qǔ
(take)

女
nǔ
(female)

娶
qǔ
(marry)

家
jiā
(home)

嫁
jià
(marry)

結
jiē
(to form)

婚
hūn
(marriage)

Once a man got a woman home, the first thing he and his family wanted from her was a male child. A son is the greatest of goods, and so the word for *woman* combined with *zǐ,* the word for *son,* creates the word *hǎo,* or *good.* The word for *son, zǐ,* sometimes means *person.* In this sense, it is sometimes added to Chinese names, as in Laozi (*Lǎo zǐ*), the founder of Daoism, China's native religion, and Confucius (*Kǒng fū zǐ*), China's most famous philosopher. There is a rough counterpart in the English surnames Anderson or Johnson, although *Lǎo zǐ* does not mean *Son of Lao* but *Lao-person.*

子
zǐ
(son or person)

好
hǎo
(good)

A pointed object is smaller at one end and larger at the other, so the Chinese word for *pointed* places *small* above *large.* Two other cleverly placed hybrids are the word for

小
xiǎo
(small)

大
dà
(large)

jiān
(pointed)

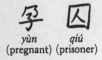

yùn (pregnant)   qiú (prisoner)

nǎo (not good)   ēn (not big)

yǒu (have)   mǎo (have not)

shàng-xià

xīn (heart)

tǎn   tè (apprehensive)

rén (man)   cóng (to follow)

mù (tree)   lín (forest)

huǒ (fire)   yán (inflammation)

pregnant, again using the word zǐ, or son, and the word prisoner, employing rén, or man. Pictorial hybrids are not always subtle. Bù, or no, plus hǎo, good, means obviously no good. Bù plus dà, big, means not big. The character for have, yǒu, has two little lines, missing in the character have not, mǎo.

Obvious or subtle, the logic cannot always be followed. The character 卡 , combining shàng, 上 , up, and xià, 下 , down, has no meaning whatsoever unless it is combined with the word for woman, nǚ. The resulting character, pronounced shàng-xià, is in the margin. Can you guess its meaning? The answer is at the bottom of the page.

In another interesting use of the characters for up and down, Chinese combine them with xīn, or heart, written twice to describe a state of extreme anxiety or trepidation.

A small group of hybrids contains characters with two or three identical parts. Repeating the same character sometimes produces an obvious meaning, sometimes not. Three examples of twin-character hybrids are shown in the margin. Hybrids of three repeating characters are more common. Some of these are shown in Table 2.3.

The word jiān, meaning adultery, again reflects Chinese male dominance. Logically, a woman's adultery should be expressed by the combination of three male characters, as shown in the margin. Such a character does

Elevator girl, or female elevator operator, is a word recently coined, showing that the process of invention is continuing. Most Chinese words are monosyllabic; this word is one of the few exceptions.

Table 2.3. Repeating Characters

Character written once means			Character repeated means		
人	rén	man	众	zhòng	crowd*
火	huǒ	fire	炎	yàn	sparks
口	kǒu	mouth	品	pǐn	conduct†
木	mù	tree, wood	森	sēn	forest
女	nǚ	female	姦	jiān	adultery, rape
石	shí	stone	磊	lěi	massive
耳	ěr	ear	聶	niè	whisper
車	chē	carriage, car	轟	hōng	rumble

*As in the English proverb, "Two's company, three's a crowd."
†Showing again the importance Chinese attach to what people say.

not exist, because of the same double standard found in the West. An active sex life with various partners is condoned, even encouraged, in males, yet a Chinese woman is supposed to remain faithful to her husband, even after his death. Obviously, some married Chinese women must have been partners in adultery, but they are relegated to nonentities by their own language.

Many fanciful histories of hybrid characters are suggested in past and present texts. Careful linguistic research into their origins has only been possible in the last fifty years, as contemporary archaeologists discover more and more from ancient inscriptions in bone and bronze.

Most compounds of two or more characters belong to a fourth category, "ideographic-phonetic." We have introduced one of these already, in the word *hūn*, marriage. One part of an "ideographic-phonetic" character is an ideographic clue to meaning, the other indicates pronunciation. Usually, the meaning indicator is on the left, while the phonetic part appears on the right.

One example of an ideographic-phonetic character is the word for *material*. The character for *tree* or *wood*, on

cái
(material)

the left, 木, is a clue to meaning, implying *material*, while the phonetic indicator 才 on the right means *just now* or *talent* when it stands alone, and is pronounced *cái*.

The character for *ocean*, pronounced *yáng*, is another illustration of an ideographic-phonetic combination. When combined with other characters, the three strokes

yáng
(ocean)

on the left frequently signify *water*, as they did when we saw them beside the pictograph for *wine*. The sound for *ocean* comes from the character on the right, 羊, which is pronounced *yáng*, and by itself carries the meaning *sheep*.

mǎ
(horse)

The word for *horse*, *mǎ*, is the phonetic indicator in

mā
(mother)

mà
(scold)

two words: *mother (mā)* and *scold (mà)*. In *mother*, the character for *woman* is a clue to meaning, as are the two mouths above the horse's head in the word for *scold*.

Chinese etymologists have identified a fifth group of characters, "phonetic loan words." Back in the days when there were more words to speak than characters to write, people would borrow an established character to write a word with a similar sound. It was as if English speakers drew a picture of a horse to represent the sound of a voice long overused.

For example, there were once two versions of the character for *scorpion*. One, showing head, tail, and claws, was pronounced *chài;* another, showing head, tail, claws, and legs, was pronounced *wan*. Another word was also spoken *wan* and meant *ten thousand* but had no written equivalent. The character for *wàn (scorpion)* was borrowed, claws, head, legs, and all, to express *ten thousand* and has now metamorphosed into the modern character for *ten thousand.**

chài

wan

wàn
(10,000)

Although contemporary Chinese seldom remember the origins of phonetic loan words, recent research into bronze inscriptions of the Zhou dynasty (ca. 1122–249 B.C.) has shown the borrowing process at work.

Certain symbols, like 木 and 氵 , which we saw earlier, recur in character after character, often revealing or suggesting meaning. These symbols are called "radicals." There are about 220 radicals, appearing in hybrid as well as ideographic-phonetic characters. A list of common radicals appears in Appendix 2.

Some radicals have an independent existence as pictographs or simple ideographs. By itself, the stylized drawing of a tree means *tree* or *wood*, as we saw. In combination, this radical gives meaning to the words for *cane*, *chair*, *table*, and *cup*.

---

*For this example we are indebted to Father L. Weiger, *Chinese Characters: Their Origin, Etymology, History, Classification, and Signification* (2nd ed. rev.) New York: Paragon Book Reprint Corp., 1965.

杖	椅	桌	杯
zhàng (cane)	*yǐ* (chair)	*zhuō* (table)	*bēi* (cup)

The character 女, discussed earlier, appears in many words related to *female*:

妹	妖	媚	妓
mèi (younger sister)	*yāo* (witch)	*mèi* (pretty)	*jì* (prostitute)

Other common radicals are 心, or *xīn* (heart):

忘	戀	怒	恥
wàng (to forget)	*liàn* (to love)	*nù* (angry)	*chī* (shame)

and 雨, or *yǔ* (rain):

雪	雷	雲	霉
xuě (snow)	*léi* (thunder)	*yún* (cloud)	*méi* (moldy)

Finally we show the radical 酉, or *yǒu*, which appears in the word for *wine*:

醉	酸	醋	酵
zuì (drunk)	*suān* (sour)	*cù* (vinegar)	*jiào* (yeast)

It is interesting to note that the English word *vinegar* is also related etymologically to *wine*, being derived from the Latin word for *wine, vīnum.*

Other radicals never stand alone, like the three-stroke ⺡ we met in the word for *ocean.* This radical cannot be pronounced, for it does not represent a spoken word. It appears in other words like *river, sea, shallow,* and *flow.*

hé	hǎi	chián	liú
(river)	(sea)	(shallow)	(flow)

Radicals can make the task of learning written Chinese much easier because they repeat in so many different words. Unfortunately, a great number of Chinese words do not have radicals that suggest meaning, or, for that matter, a phonetic indicator.

All Chinese characters are built from strokes of the brush or pen, and their structure may seem forbiddingly complicated to a beginner. Actually, a small number of strokes, pictured in Table 2.4, are used in all characters. For contrast, look at the basic lines used to form the letters of the Western alphabet, shown below.

. ( ) — / \ | ∩ ∪

We will say more about the differences between handwriting, East and West, in Chapter 7.

Table 2.4. Basic Strokes for Chinese Characters

Lines		*Angles*	
Horizontal line:	—	Right angle:	㇆
Vertical line:	│	Acute angle:	㇆ ㇄
Dots	丶 '	Obtuse angle:	㇔
Sweeps		*Hooks*	
Long sweeps:	) ㇄ │	Horizontal:	→
Short sweeps:	' '	Vertical:	│ │
		Curve hooks:	㇆ ㇄) ㇄

Table 2.5. Some Look-Alike Characters

人	入		天	夭	夫
rèn	*rù*		*tiān*	*yāo*	*fú*
(man)	(to enter)		(sky)	(to die young)	(husband)

大	犬	太	王	玉	主
dà	*quǎn*	*tài*	*wáng*	*yù*	*zhǔ*
(large)	(dog)	(too much)	(king)	(jade)	(master)

己	已	巳		土	士
jǐ	*yǐ*	*sì*		*tǔ*	*shì*
(self)	(already)	(9–11 A.M.)		(soil)	(scholar)

田	由	曲	甲	申	电
tián	*yóu*	*qǔ*	*jiǎ*	*shēn*	*diàn*
(field)	(from)	(a song)	(an armor)	(3–5 P.M.)	(electricity)

Table 2.6. Some Frames for Analyzing Chinese Characters

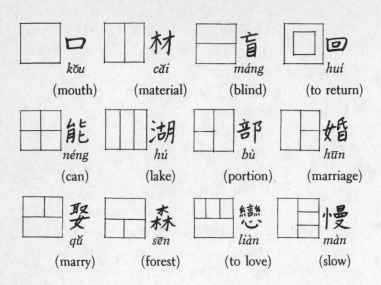

Each character must contain a precise number of strokes, written in the proper order. *Zì*, or *character*, is composed of six strokes written in the sequence shown below.

| Dot | Sweep | Horizontal sweep | Acute angle | Curve hook | Horizontal line |

The misplacement of a tiny dot can completely alter the meaning of a sentence, causing confusion or embarrassment. Some look-alike characters are pictured in Table 2.5.

Frames help beginning writers of Chinese to properly

一
yī
(one)

合
hě
(box)

酥
sū
(crisp candy)

一
yī
(one)

人
rèn
(man)

一
yī
(one)

口
kǒu
(mouth)

酥
sū
(crisp candy)

place each part of a character. Table 2.6 shows some of the common frames together with word examples.

Calligraphers eschew these symmetrical frames and use the ninefold square pictured in Chapter 7 as a guide for composing characters.

In the old days, when Chinese was always written vertically, one could on occasion play games with words. The following story is taken from *The Three Kingdoms*, peopled with emperors and generals who fought battles around the third century of the Christian era. Once a prime minister of the Han dynasty (202 B.C.–220 A.D.) received a box of crisp candy (a real delicacy in those days) from a northern province. Not wishing to eat it all at once, he wrote *yī hě sū, one box of crisp candy,* on the outside of the box and then put it away. One of his subordinates, a bright and cocky scholar, noticed the writing and immediately shared the candy among his colleagues. When confronted by his master, the scholar replied facetiously that they were only following his order. Since the middle word may be broken down into three separate words (see margin), the sentence could just as well read: *Each person a mouthful of crisp candy.* Everyone laughed at this explanation, including the prime minister, who was really not amused by the scholar's insolence. A few years later, he found a suitable excuse to have the young smart aleck beheaded.

Learning to read and write Chinese requires years of patient practice for Western adults and Chinese children alike. Before 1949, the education of wealthy boys and girls began around the age of seven. Most likely, the first book they encountered was *Sàn zì jīng,* the *Three Character Classic.* They used it as generations of colonial children used their *New England Primer,* to learn elementary reading skills along with the philosophy fundamental to their culture. While Chinese children of the Qing dynasty (1644–1912) A.D.) were poring over the first words of the *Three Character Classic,*

三
sàn
(three)

字
zì
(character)

經
jīng
(classic)

人	自	初	性	本	善
rèn	*zì*	*chū*	*xìng*	*běn*	*shàn*
(man)	(since)	(beginning)	(nature)	(origin)	(good)

or "Men at their birth are naturally good," English-speaking children were reading rhymed couplets for each letter of the alphabet, beginning with "A/ In Adam's fall/We sinned all," a poem that appeared in countless primers published in England and America during the eighteenth century (Figure 2.1).

Chinese children, like their American counterparts before the twentieth century, learned writing by copying and reading by recitation. Sometimes young scholars had only the vaguest idea of what they were reading or writing. Fortunately, their curriculum also included reading lessons from simple primers using characters for familiar words. Slowly, more characters were added, until a child could read and comprehend a simple story.

文
wén
(literature)

言
yán
(speech)

The next phase of traditional aristocratic education introduced *wényán,* or classical Chinese, again employing

Fig. 2.1. "In *Adam's* Fall/We sinned all." From an English primer, 1725.

rote memorization as the main teaching method. Students would learn three or four pages of a classical text by heart. The teacher expected pupils to recite the passage or copy it in acceptable calligraphy, but never to understand or explain it.

For most children of the 1920s and 1930s, the last phase of Chinese education involved writing original compositions using everyday vocabulary. Rarely, a student would emulate his grandfather and continue his education long enough to master *wényán*. In centuries past, when bureaucrats were selected by nationwide examinations, no man was really educated unless he could compose graceful essays in *wényán*, and, of course, write them in striking calligraphy. More about *wényán* and calligraphy in later chapters.

By now, the most practical of our readers must be

asking: Wouldn't it be better to scrap the characters, however wise and artistic, for a simple phonetic alphabet reflecting the sounds of spoken Chinese? Many linguists and politicians have asked this question since the beginning of this century, when Chinese intellectuals realized that their country's survival depended on compromising aesthetic and intellectual standards in order to adopt more efficient Western ways.

Both Chinese and Western linguists devised systems of *Romanization,* expressing the sounds of spoken Chinese in the Roman letters of the Western alphabet. Besides helping Westerners learn Chinese, Romanization facilitates the spread of literacy in China. Table 2.7 shows how four Romanizations in current use treat the sentence "There are many people in China" and the words "Northern Capital." Note that not all Romanizers hear Chinese the same way.

Table 2.7. Various Forms of Romanization

Chinese	中國	人	多	北京
English	China	man	many	Northern Capital
Wade-Giles	*Chūngkuo*	*jen*	*tō*	*Peking*
Gwoyeu Romantzyh	*Jonhhwo*	*ren*	*dwo*	*Peiping**
Yale	*Jūnggwo*	*rén*	*dwō*	*Beijing*
Pīnyīn	*Zhōngguó*	*rén*	*duō*	*Beijing*

*This pronunciation is for 北平, for many years the name used by the Nationalists for the Northern Capital.

The oldest and most widespread Romanization in current use is Wade-Giles. In 1842, Sir Thomas Francis Wade, a lieutenant in the British infantry, first set foot in China. A man of action on both military and diplomatic fronts during the turbulent years of the mid-nineteenth century when European powers forced concession after concession from China, Wade found time to learn Chinese and collect a valuable library. In 1888, he retired to a chair at Cambridge University, where he introduced the study of Chinese. His system of Romanization, first published in his *Peking Syllabary* (1859), was perfected by his successor at Cambridge, Herbert Allen Giles, a parson's son and career diplomat, whose contributions to Anglo-Chinese relations were purely intellectual. A prolific writer and translator, Giles did more than anyone else of his time to popularize Chinese literature and culture.

In the 1930s, two American-educated scholars of the Chinese Republic, Lin Yu-tang and Chao Yuen-ren, conceived and developed a different way of spelling Chinese words, one that reflected the tonal aspect of Chinese. (We will discuss tones in the next chapter.) The result was *Gwoyeu Romantzyh*, or "National Romanization," still used by the Republic of China on Taiwan.

Until the Second World War, most Westerners who studied Chinese learned only to read and write. They might be able to translate *wényán* into English, but not to carry on a conversation. The Second World War created an immediate need for servicemen fluent in Chinese. Scholars at Yale University, which in 1871 had introduced the teaching of Chinese in America, created an intensive program for Air Force pilots who needed to speak, not write, Chinese. This pioneer program involved frequent contact with native speakers and long daily sessions in a language laboratory.

Since the emphasis was upon speaking, Roman letters were substituted for Chinese characters. A new system of Romanization was developed, keyed to the American accent. After the war, the university published a series of textbooks using Yale Romanization, still the most successful in reproducing the sounds of Chinese for the American tongue. Updated versions of these texts are used for college-level teaching of Chinese all over America.

Pīnyīn is the style of Romanization used throughout this book, except for widely recognized proper names and places. It is rooted in a Romanization developed by Soviet scholars and is a tool for the campaign against illiteracy in the People's Republic of China. It is even adopted to a certain extent by the government on Taiwan. In China, as in other countries, language is intimately connected with politics, as we shall see when we explore the history of the Chinese language.

Three

SPOKEN CHINESE

zì
(character)

Chinese speakers use words of one syllable, or *zì*, as building blocks for polysyllabic words, phrases, and sentences. When compared with many other languages, including English, Chinese places very few sounds at the disposal of its speakers. Mandarin allows four hundred spoken one-syllable words, approximately; Cantonese makes about twice that number available. With so few building blocks, how can Chinese construct linguistic structures equal to the complexities of human life?

One way is to employ single words for many jobs. The Chinese vocabulary includes quantities of homonyms, words with similar sounds but different meanings. When an American carpenter has bored too many holes in a board and is bored with his work, he may write to the Chairman of the Board. A spoken Chinese sentence could include a dozen such puns. The same word, *mai,* means both *buy* and *sell; ming* is *dark* or *bright; ma, mother* or *horse.* Among dozens of translations for the word *shi* are *poetry, pig, nuthatch, corpse, use, beginning, affair, to try, history.* With so many words that sound alike but carry different meanings, how do Chinese ever understand one another? When a farmer tells his friend he took his mother to town, how does the friend know his companion was not his horse? Now, all these various meanings are written differently, so *readers* are not confused. Chinese speakers have another trick that sometimes dumbfounds Westerners: they speak in tones.

With no exact counterparts in English, tones are hard to describe. Basically, they are differences in the pitch of each spoken syllable. Chinese speakers use tones so automatically that they sometimes have difficulty explaining them. Tones are what give the Chinese language its distinctive singsong quality.

Ancient Chinese was enhanced by eight tonal variations. Cantonese retains all eight of these tones, while Mandarin has kept only four. To get a rough idea of how these four tones sound, imagine a conversation between two boys.

Jeremy has climbed on a garbage can to peep through the back window of a pet shop, closed on a Sunday morning.

"What do you see?" asks his friend Aaron.

"Dogs," answers Jeremy.

"Dogs?" repeats Aaron, his voice rising in query.

"Not dogs!" He is unable to believe his ears.

"That's all I see," protests Jeremy.

"Dogs," sighs Aaron, who was hoping to catch a glimpse of the boa constrictor his older brother saw last Thursday.

Each pronunciation of the word *dogs* in the exchange above illustrates a tone in Mandarin. When Jeremy says "dogs" the first time, he is stating a fact. His voice keeps the even pitch of the first tone. The second, or rising, tone sounds like an American asking a question. A word pronounced in the third tone dips down and then rises up, similar to the pitch of Aaron's "Not dogs," while a word in the fourth tone falls straight down, as in Aaron's expression of disappointment.

When Chinese want to demonstrate Mandarin's four tones, they often use four meanings of the word *ma* as follows:

mā	(even tone)	mother	媽
má	(rising tone)	hemp	麻
mǎ	(dipping tone)	horse	馬
mà	(falling tone)	scold	罵

Pīnyīn indicates tone by placing an accent mark over one vowel, a straight line for the even tone, an acute accent for the rising tone, a curved line for the dipping tone, and a grave accent for the falling tone.

The characters for the four meanings of *ma* show the phonetic loan process at work, creating ideographic-phonetic characters. Originally, the pictograph for *horse* was pronounced *mǎ*. Gradually, this character was adopted for other words pronounced *ma*, and written beside another character that indicated meaning.

And now, the inevitable tongue twister that is heard whenever the different meanings of *ma* are introduced:

Māmā* qí mǎ   Mǎ màn   Māmā mà   mǎ

媽媽騎馬　馬慢媽媽罵馬

Mother rides horse　Horse slow　Mother scolds horse

In normal conversation, Chinese speakers do not give a tone to every word in a sentence. Words resembling the English articles, prepositions, and conjunctions are spoken neutrally. Words in a compound do not always retain their special tones. In general, the tonal pitch is applied to words the speakers want to emphasize.

Musicians may be interested in knowing how tones are used in Chinese songs. A Chinese operatic dialogue is sung, and its meaning is important to the audience, so tones must be retained, even in arias. The score is arranged so that musical tones do not conflict with linguistic ones.

Singing or speaking, a person must be careful with tones, or he could find himself in trouble, even with the best of intentions. To say to an artist in his studio, *"Wǒ yào mài yīzhāng hùar,"* "I want to sell a painting," could

買
mǎi
(buy)

*The child's word for *mother* is the same in English and Chinese.

cause a flare-up of artistic temper, and an embellished equivalent of "Don't come to me, you skinflint," a reply puzzling to the American art lover who thought he had said, "I want to buy a painting." *("Wǒ yào mǎi yīzhāng huàr.")*

mài
(sell)

An English speaker learning Chinese would do well not to flounder in the morass of diacritical marks and other notations, like superscript numbers in some versions of the Wade-Giles Romanization, nor should he try to memorize lists of words spoken in a neutral tone. The best course is to listen carefully to native speakers and concentrate on the separate sound for each meaning. This is the way an American child learns his own language; until a foreigner mentions it, he may never realize that a small shade of emphasis separates the noun *minute*, a unit of time, from the adjective *minute*, very small.

Some Chinese words, like *mǐn'it* and *mī-nōōt*, are written exactly alike but pronounced differently. The character in the margin means *can* when pronounced *huì* and *accounting* when pronounced *kuài*.

會

中 國
zhōng *guó*
(middle) (kingdom)

Many of the 25,000 or so individual *zì* are combined to create compounds perceived as single words. *Zhōng,* middle, and *guó, kingdom,* hitch together to make *Zhōngguó, Middle Kingdom,* the name Chinese call their homeland.

明 天
míng *tiān*
(bright) (sky)

吃 飯
chī *fàn*
(eat) (rice)

A *zì* may or may not retain its original meaning when joined in a compound. The word *míng* by itself means *clear* or *bright. Tiān* alone means *sky.* The compound *míngtiān* means *tomorrow,* not always a bright sky. A beginner might read the combination of *chī, eat,* and *fàn, rice*, as *eat rice*, but it translates simply as *eat*. The same is true of *shuōhuà*, formed of *shuō*, *to speak*, and *huà*, *language*. Words that spoken Chinese joins together can always stand by themselves. Chinese has no equivalent of Western prefixes like *de-* or *anti-*, and suffixes like *-logy* or *-ism*, word pieces that never stand alone.

説　話
shuō　*huà*
(to speak) (language)

Chinese almost never permits direct borrowing of foreign words, and fortunately avoids such barbarisms as the French *le hamburger*. When new words do come from lands beyond the seas, the Chinese have two ways of coping. One course is to translate into Chinese words. The other option is to transliterate, by representing the sounds of Western words in equivalent Chinese characters. *Rocket* is translated into *huǒjiàn*, or *fire arrow*, as is *airplane*, *fēijī*, or *flying machine*. *Chocolate* is transliterated as *qiǎo-kě-lì*, a compound that could mean *cleverly gives you strength*, or could be nonsense, depending on the interpretation of each *zì*.

Sometimes translation and transliteration are felicitously combined. *Coca-Cola* is *kě-kǒu-kě-lè* in Chinese, a phrase meaning *soothes the mouth and brings joy to the drinker*. The Beatles, adored in the mid-1960s by rock music enthusiasts from Haverhill to Hong Kong, were called by their Chinese fans *Pītóu*, or *hair around the shoulders*.

Foreign names are almost always transliterated. Clinton is *Ke Lin-deng* and Bush is *Bu shen* or *xiǎo Bu shen* (small or younger Bush) to distinguish him from his father.

Chinese does not have a sound for *r*. *Europe* rolls off the tongue as *Eulope*. *Grass* is often pronounced *glass*.

Words do not travel in just one direction, from West to East, for English has its share of words borrowed from Chinese. *Coolie,* for example, comes from the Mandarin *kūlì, bitter strength,* a clear description of the backbreaking physical labor performed by poor workers. *Kowtow* is a corruption of Mandarin's *kòutòu, knock-head* (against the floor). *Jinrickshaw* or *rickshaw* derives from a three-word compound *rénlìchē,* or *man-strength-vehicle.* The word is outmoded on the Mainland, where rickshaws no longer exist because it is considered degrading for one human being to pull another.

The Mandarin word *zásuì, mixed pieces,* became *chop suey* in English. The dish is strictly an American invention. Another all-American food, hamburger, is not really complete without ketchup, a condiment that bears little resemblance to its namesake *ketsiap,* which is what the people of Amoy, an island off the coast of Fukien, called pickled fish sauce. Everyone knows tea comes from China, and so, of course, does the word. While northern Chinese spoke of *chá,* seventeenth-century Dutch traders, who introduced tea to the West, listened to the tea merchants in Amoy and heard the drink called *te,* which, twisted around the Dutch tongue, became *thee,* and eventually traveled to England as *tea.*

A popular American game, Mah-Jongg, is also enjoyed by overseas Chinese. Walking along Mott Street in New York's Chinatown on a summer night, you will hear, if you listen carefully, the click of ivory tiles from the open windows above, evidence of a game in progress. The word comes from the Cantonese pronunciation of Mandarin's *má jiāng, spotted sparrow,* pictured on one of the tiles.

Pidgin English, described by the noted linguist Mario Pei as a kind of baby talk for adults, grew up around southern Chinese ports in the seventeenth century. Simplified English words, pronounced with a heavy Cantonese accent, were grafted onto Chinese grammatical structure to create a hybrid language of trade that trailed out across the Pacific, shooting off varieties of pidgin used in Melanesia, New Guinea, Tahiti, and Samoa. The pidgin English rooted in China has given Americans a lively collection of slang words. *Gung ho,* an English phrase meaning *foolishly eager,* comes from Mandarin *gōng hé,* or *work together.* The Mandarin *ji, fast, hurried,* pronounced *kap* in Cantonese, became *chop-chop* in English, or *hurry, hurry!* Chinese boatmen, familiar figures to English traders, refused to use the regular Chinese word, *zhu,* to describe the long, pointed sticks they used to eat their rice. *Zhu* was a homonym for *stop,* or *stand still,* an unlucky word on the river, so the boatmen called their eating utensils *kuài zí,* a Mandarin expression for *fast ones.* This word was permanently adopted into the Chinese language and entered pidgin as *chopsticks,* or *fast sticks.* The word *pidgin* itself is a corruption of the English word *business.*

English is also enriched by loan translations, phrases literally translated from the Chinese. *Miàn zǐ,* or *save face,* is such a loan translation, and so is *brainwash,* from the Chinese phrase *xǐnǎo,* wash-brain, a technique of political reeducation. When Philip Marlowe, the fictional private detective played by Humphrey Bogart, says "Let's have a look-see," he seems to be using a phrase that directly translates the Chinese word *kànjiàn*, a compound of *kàn*, *look*, and *jiàn*, *see*, properly translated *to see*. *Old hand* probably comes from the Chinese phrase *lǎo shǒu (old hand)*, or *expert*.

An interesting tale of Occidental ideas about China hangs on the word *mandarin*, meaning a senior official the Chinese called *guān*. *Mandarin* has no Chinese origins whatsoever. Because the seventeenth-century rulers of China wanted to keep foreigners at a distance, the Portuguese who made commercial contacts then were not allowed to learn their language. Not knowing the correct name, they called the officials they dealt with *Mandarins*, from the Malay verb *to order*, a word with Sanskrit roots grown from the same Indo-European stock as Portuguese and English. Enlightenment philosophers of the eighteenth century conceived of China as an ideal government ruled by men selected for wisdom and education; to them *Mandarin* was a term of respect. Today it carries the more sinister connotation of a bureaucrat with great power, power undefined and uncontrolled.

Fluid and simple, Chinese grammar is not governed by the immutable laws drawn up to bedevil students of Western languages. The basic structure of a Chinese sentence is

Subject ⟶ verb ⟶ object

If one of these components is dropped, the sentence can still be correct. The flexibility of Chinese frequently unnerves beginners, who badger the Chinese teacher with questions like "Why are the words in this order?" and expect to learn a clear-cut rule they can apply in similar situations. The teacher, not wishing to confuse with rules complicated by their very flexibility, may reply inscrutably, "No reason, they just are." After a period of frustration, the student listens to sentence patterns and tries to understand the generalizations he can make about Chinese.

A novice longs to put the new words he is learning into neat pigeonholes labeled *noun, verb, adjective,* and so on. Verbs, adjectives, adverbs, and other familiar parts of speech are found in the Chinese language, but words keep changing pigeonholes, especially verbs and adjectives. For example, *hǎo* is an adjective meaning *good* as well as a verb meaning *to be good.* To complicate matters, a textbook may use exotic phrases like *functive verb, movable verb,* and *resultative verb,* to categorize parts of speech that are uniquely Chinese.

Chinese has no article like the English *the,* but uses *this* and *these* instead. Chinese learning English find mastering *the* difficult. Their teachers may find it stuck in without reason, or missing completely when it should be there.

One of the first words a student of Mandarin learns is *tā,* translated as *he, she, it, him,* or *her.* There is a different written character for male, female, and neuter forms, but spoken Chinese makes no such distinction as to gender. Because of this, Chinese who speak English as a second language may come out with mistakes like, *My girl friend lost his purse.* A Westerner may wonder if using the same word for *he* and *she, him* and *her* causes confusion. The Chinese would explain that *tā* gains meaning from the context of the conversation.

Two other grammatical features of Western languages not found in Chinese are plural nouns and verb tenses. *Rén (man)* does not change whether it means one man or a hundred men. Chinese nouns are usually preceded by a classifier which makes the number clear. The sentence *Wǒ mǎi shū* can be translated:

I buy books.
I am buying books.
I bought books.
I was buying books.
I had bought books.
I have bought books.
I have been buying books.
I will buy books.
I will be buying books.
I will have bought books.

The noun *books* could just as easily be translated *book* because, as explained above, Chinese nouns do not have a plural or singular form. Again, Chinese speakers rely on context to prevent confusion. A time word can be inserted before the verb, as in the sentence *Zuótiān wǒ mǎi shū, Yesterday I bought books,* or *Míngtiān wǒ yào mǎi shū, Tomorrow I will buy books.* The word *yào* means *want, must,* or *will.*

Knowing all this, try to imagine how a Chinese would

say, *If I knew then what I know now, would I have done what I did?*

Of course, the Chinese ask themselves this question as often as the rest of mankind does, but they must use more words to do it.

When an American searches Chinese for familiar features of Western grammar, he will discover some completely new grammatical distinctions. One is a means of clarifying verb tenses without resorting to words like *last week* or *next year*. In Chinese grammar, it is not so important to know when an action occurred. Instead, the Chinese concentrate on a change in status or the completion of an action. The particle *le* (pronounced tonelessly) in a sentence indicates change or completion. It is called *functive* because, like *the,* it never stands on its own, and has to be used in conjunction with other words.

To say *Tā hǎo, She good,* means *She is well.* Adding *le* to the sentence, *Tā hǎo le, She good le,* changes the meaning to *She has recovered,* for *le* implies a change in status. She is well now but has not always been so. *Le* tacked onto the sentence *Tā lái, He comes,* suggests an action completed. *Tā lái le, He comes le,* translates, according to context, *He came, He has come,* or *He had come.* Sometimes *le* is used in connection with a changed situation to indicate determination. For example, the sentence *Wǒ bù yào le* means *I don't want it!* (Before this situation had changed, I thought I might want it.) It can also be used in command or request, as in *Nǐ kàn shū le,* meaning *You read books!* or *Will you read books?*

Chinese contains many vivid expressions created by

陰 陽

yīn *yáng*

pairing opposites. Daoism, an ancient Chinese philoso-phy, described two opposite forces called *yīn* and *yáng*, encompassing dark and light, female and male, passive and active, death and birth. On a more mundane level, abstract nouns are expressed by combining *zì* of opposite meanings. Some examples are: *chángduǎn, long-short*, for *length, dàxiǎo, big-small*, for *size, lěngrè, cold-hot*, for *temperature*, and *mǎimài, buy-sell*, for *business* or *shop*.

The Chinese commonly ask questions by juxtaposing opposites. *Nǐ ài bù ài wǒ* means literally *You love not love me* and is properly translated *Do you love me?* The appo-sition of positive and negative statements is one of two ways to frame a question in Chinese. The other is to hitch the word *ma* to the end of a statement.

The interrogative particle *ma* is the Chinese equiva-lent of a question mark. Using *ma*, the question *Do you love me?* would be *Nǐ ài wǒ ma*, literally *You love me ma*. Incidentally, question marks are printed in Chinese texts, often following the word *ma*. Question marks and other marks of punctuation were recently borrowed from West-ern languages, much to the dismay of classical Chinese scholars, who regard them as superfluous barbarian squig-gles defacing refined calligraphy.

The Chinese equivalent of an English apostrophe *s*, indicating possession, is another functive called *de*, as in *tāde māo, his cat*, or *hóuzide wěiba*, the *monkey's tail*. Chinese gets more grammatical mileage out of the posses-sive sense than does English. *De* is frequently applied to whole phrases or sentences, as *Zài fēijī lǐ de rén kàn bù jiàn wǒ*, literally *Inside the airplane's man cannot see me*, or *The man inside the airplane cannot see me.*

Chinese sentence patterns are marked by a tendency to move from general to specific, from large to small. In written dates, the year comes first, then the month, then the day. Fractions are expressed with the whole first: *five percent* is *băi-fēn-shùr-wŭ*, or *hundred-fraction-five* literally. To say *One of those two pretty girls is engaged*, a Chinese must state *Those two pretty girls, one of them is engaged (Nā liăng gè hăo kān de nŭ hái zĭ, yŏu yī gĕ shì dĭng le hūn).* This sentence illustrates another interesting use of *de* as a word modifying an adjective, making it possessive in relation to the following noun. *Two pretty girls* in Chinese would be written *two pretty's girls.*

Although a student may find unpluralized Chinese nouns ambiguous at first, he soon realizes that they are amplified by "classifiers." Classifiers are found in English: a *piece* of paper, for example, or a *loaf* of bread. Chinese has many more and is very strict about linking a noun with its proper classifier, although a limited set of classifiers work for a large number of nouns. Some examples of classifiers are:

個 for person or persons,
week, month, etc.
gĕ

些 for people or articles
(number is not specified)
xiē

隻 for boat, pen, etc.
zhī

塊　for stone, dollar, bread, etc.

kuài

張　for bed, paper, etc.

zhāng

As in English, there is no logic behind the choice. A beginner has to memorize these, just as foreigners learning English have to get used to phrases like *a flock of birds, several bundles of laundry,* and so on.

Chinese sentences are full of discontinuous constituents. Familiar English examples of this grammatical feature are *either . . . or, not only . . . but also,* and *on one hand . . . on the other.* Chinese includes *kě shì . . . bù néng (but . . . cannot) zài . . . qián tóu (in front of . . .), yīn wèi . . . yuán gù (owing to . . .),* and so on. Splitting up phrases this way makes translation more difficult.

没

méi
(no, not)

不

bù
(no, not)

Two words are used as negative particles: *méi* and *bù,* each in a different situation. The word *méi* is always used with the verb *yǒu,* meaning *to have* or *there is,* while *bù* is used to negate all other verbs. The following two sentences do not have exactly the same meanings: *Tā bù qù* means *He does not go,* whereas *Tā méi yǒu qù* means *He has not gone.*

There is an interesting difference between the ways Chinese and English-speaking people use the affirmative and negative. Let us suppose that a novice in tennis is asked the question "Haven't you learned the slice serve yet?" by his father, who is paying for the lessons. If he has not, then the answer in English would be "No. I have not." However, a similar situation in Chinese would result in the reply "Yes. I have not." The word *yes* here refers to the fact that he has not yet learned the slice serve. Chinese speaking English often carry over this usage, causing confusion and bewilderment to their American friends.

Without a phonetic alphabet to solidify its sounds, spoken Chinese is relatively fluid, permitting more latitude in pronunciation than Western languages. This is one reason why the various Romanizations mentioned in Chapter 2 have such different spellings for the same word. Clues to past pronunciation of Chinese words are few and far between. The best that linguistic historians can do is to study early writings on language and read ancient poetry. Many words that do not sound alike in modern Chinese once rhymed.

Although the past of spoken Chinese must remain largely uncharted, written Chinese has a long, abundantly documented history, as the next chapter will show.

Four

IT ALL STARTED WITH DRAGON BONES: A SHORT HISTORY OF THE CHINESE LANGUAGE

The beginning of the twentieth century was a low point in Chinese history. Drought, famine, and disease prostrated the common people. Opium addiction spread, and the government was powerless to stop it, for British guns protected the drug's importers.* Pulled by a nose ring of

*The Opium War was one of the cruelest chapters in China's degradation at the hands of the West. To many Westerners, China has always been a nation of opium smokers. This was indeed true before the Communists took over the Mainland in 1949, yet few people know the facts about the importation of opium into China. Although small quantities of opium had been used medicinally in China since ancient times, the first large quantities were brought to China by Portugal at the beginning of the eighteenth century. In later years, opium poppies were grown in India, where, under careful and efficient British management, large quantities of opium were harvested and shipped under the protection of the British navy to seaports in southern China. By the mid-nineteenth century, the annual import of opium amounted to about four

economic dominance held by countries once relegated to a "Bureau of Barbarian Affairs," China was forced to bow before superior weaponry and technology.

Even worse, a bulwark of cultural tradition three thousand years old was crumbling beneath the impact of Western scientific thought, further demoralizing Chinese intellectuals. Chinese writers published articles claiming that their own people were inherently incapable of operating foreign machines, let alone inventing new ones. A mood of self-doubt, of dissatisfaction with old wisdom, extended into every branch of study.

Goaded by Occidental standards for scientific proof, Chinese historians scrutinized their ancient records with increased skepticism. Were the stirring histories of the earliest dynasties Yin and Zhou only legends? Were there enough hard facts to prove that Confucius really lived? Some Western scholars even chipped away at the foundation stone of Chinese culture, its written language, by suggesting that Chinese characters were not native to the

---

million pounds! Alarmed by the enormously damaging effects of the drug on the minds and bodies of his subjects, the emperor Daoguang strove to break "the British Connection" in 1838 by ordering one of his ablest servants, Lin Zexu, to put an end to the import of opium. After arriving in Guangzhou, Lin confiscated all the opium in the possession of foreign traders and had it publicly burned. However, he was unable to extract a pledge that no future shipments of opium would be made. Angered by the traders' arrogant refusal, Lin threatened to ban all foreign commercial traffic. Britain had planned a war against China for quite some time, in order to gain more trade concessions, and this incident provided a timely excuse for her to fire the first shot. The Opium War was over quickly, for China had no defense against British guns. In the Treaty of Nanking (1842), which ended the war, China was forced to open five ports to British trade, cede the island of Hong Kong to Great Britain, and pay indemnity for the opium confiscated. And the opium trade continued as before, bringing with it the destruction of human life that friends and relatives of present-day heroin addicts could well understand.

Middle Kingdom but had been imported from the Middle East in ages long past.

Less than a century before, in Europe, the same spirit of rational skepticism convinced scholars that Troy, a city immortalized in two thousand years of stirring tales, existed only in the poet Homer's imagination. A teen-age Heinrich Schliemann's excitement at hearing a drunkard recite Homer's *Iliad* in the original Greek turned into a lifelong obsession that carried Schliemann at last to Turkey. There, digging through a rubble of potsherds and gold, he lifted the lid from a stack of cities piled above the actual site of the Trojan War.

A small coincidence, akin to Schliemann's overhearing the drunken recitation of Homeric Greek, struck a spark that would slowly blossom into a light brilliant enough to illuminate the dim reaches of Chinese history. Here, then, is the story of this coincidence.

The farmers around the village of Xiaotun near Anyang in northern Henan Province sometimes earned a few extra copper coins from a most unusual crop: pieces of bone turned up by the plow or by heavy rain. One of these bones is shown in Figure 4.1. It was well known then that a dragon sheds its bones as a snake sheds its skin. Dragons have always played a starring role in Chinese folklore, religion, and philosophy.

To the common mind, dragons are generally benign creatures (unlike the Western dragon, which is pictured as an evil monster in league with the Devil) associated with rain, rivers, and mists, and with the emperor. Daoism, a native Chinese religion rooted in the simple

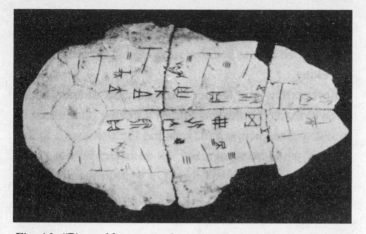

Fig. 4.1. "Piece of bone turned up by the plow . . ." (Courtesy of the Academia Sinica)

philosophy of Laozi, an older contemporary of Confucius, later developed a complex mythology featuring the dragon as a mystical force of cosmic power who appears for a moment to fill man with awe, then disappears into the mist. The Buddhist sect called *chan* in China and better known in the West by its Japanese name, Zen, elevates the dragon to a philosophical symbol for the flash of Truth that comes to enlighten the meditator. Traditional healers believed that ground-up dragon bones could cure woman's diseases, dysentery, and malaria, as well as a number of other maladies.

The farmers of Xiaotun could not be sure the bones they found came from dragons. Some had strange symbols scratched on them. Crosses and straight and curved lines could be deciphered, and even sketchy pictures. Might dragon bones bear these marks? Probably not. But the apothecaries in Beijing wanted dragon bones, and the farmers needed cash to improve their wretched lives, so they scraped off the peculiar markings and sent the bones to Beijing.

Fortunately, one farmer was a careless scraper, and a piece of marked bone was sold by a Beijing pharmacist to an indisposed antiquarian. Imagine the sick man's astonishment when he recognized, on an object he was about to grind up for medicinal broth, a written message from China's mythical past!

The year was 1899. Tantalized by the mysterious "dragon bone" hieroglyphics, a small group of Chinese scholars and antiquarians collected quantities of inscribed bones from the fields around Xiaotun, paying the farmers not in copper but in silver. Five years passed before enough symbols could be deciphered to reveal the true nature of the "dragon bones."

They were a record of a people who called themselves Shang, and ruled lands surrounding Anyang some four thousand years ago. Here was objective proof for the existence of a dynasty called "Yin" (ca. 1766 — ca. 1122 B.C.) by its Zhou conquerors, part of a heroic epoch of Chinese history, chronicled until then only in semi-legendary histories.

The objects embedded in the fields of Xiaotun came not from dragons but from tortoises and cattle. Shang kings sought to learn the future through their diviners, who inscribed royal questions on a carefully scraped and polished tortoise shell or ox shoulder blade or leg bone. The inscribed oracle shells and bones were partially drilled in prescribed patterns. Heat was applied, and the course of the resulting cracks, determined by ancestral spirits, indicated answers to their questions.

Shang oracle bones provide intriguing glimpses of life in China four millennia past. Kings then yearned to know the results of imminent military campaigns and hunting expeditions. They asked spirits to forecast the weather, the sex of children in queenly wombs, the outcome of diseases plaguing the royal family. Yet Shang oracle bones raise more questions than they answer. Like a tiny flashlight played over a dark, cavernous room filled with unknown objects, they give us a fragmented understanding of the Shang people.

Methodical excavation in Anyang district began almost thirty years after the bones were first identified. When Western scholars learned about oracle bones, they were as excited as their Chinese counterparts had been. The *New York Times* ran stories announcing their "discovery"—three decades after the fact. In the years between 1928, when excavation near Anyang began, and 1937, when invading Japanese halted the work, Chinese archaeologists unearthed a splendid Shang city, filled with treasures from China's Bronze Age. The Shang dynasty's major artistic symbol is the intricately decorated bronze vessel, cast with a skill never surpassed by succeeding generations of bronzeworkers, including the famous Renaissance artist Benvenuto Cellini. Figures 4.2 and 4.3 show two superb examples of Shang bronzework. Figure 4.2 is a square ceremonial container covered with elaborate decorations from the early thirteenth century B.C.,

Fig. 4.2. Bronze vessel of the Shang dynasty. (Courtesy of the Academia Sinica)

Fig. 4.3. Shang bronze vessel in the shape of a rhinoceros. (Asian Art Museum of San Francisco. The Avery Brundage Collection)

while Figure 4.3 is a realistic portrait of a rhinoceros from the eleventh century B.C.

When Japanese troops pushed the Nationalist government of Chiang Kai-shek from Beijing to Chongqing in 1938, Chinese archaeologists followed with carloads of artifacts, including thousands of oracle bones. These were later shipped to Taiwan, where scholars who may never again set foot on the Mainland of their own country studied the material unearthed in one decade at Anyang for the rest of their lives.

Meanwhile, in the People's Republic of China Communist leaders needed several years to deal with their desperate present before they could begin to think about the past. When archaeological excavations began anew, different conditions prevailed. No longer do ancient artifacts travel directly from farmers' fields to homes of wealthy private collectors. Today, anyone who unearths an ancient object while constructing a building or cultivating the land reports his find immediately. A team of archaeologists arrives at a promising site; excavation is a job shared between scholar and worker alike.

The success of this cooperation was clearly demonstrated by the stunning Exhibition of Archaeological Finds of the People's Republic of China, mounted first in Paris, sent on to London, Washington, Kansas City, and finally to San Francisco. There, in the summer of 1975, over three hundred thousand people viewed the exhibition. An article in the *San Francisco Chronicle* described the crowd as a varied lot, with a few more Asian faces than one might see on an average street.

The reaction of these Chinese Americans, many descended from railroad coolies and laundrymen, others recent immigrants consigned to menial jobs, was described in the same article by an Asian Art Museum employee:

> All these old Chinese men, these young Chinese chicks and guys. It's fantastic! They come here thinking, may be they're freaks, and they leave, wow, you should see their expressions. I mean this is THEIRS, man. THEIRS!*

甲
jiā
(shell)

骨
gū
(bone)

書
shū
(book)

People's Republic archaeologists uncovered thousands more Shang oracle bones. Corps of learned people created a whole new branch of linguistic study, *Jiā gū shū*, the study of shell and bone writing. As scholars pored over the writings of ancient diviners, they reached a provocative conclusion: Shang writing was not the oldest Chinese writing, not by a thousand years at least. The characters used then were already so sophisticated that they undoubtedly had many centuries of development behind them.

Very little is known about pre-Shang writing. Many cultures identify a sacred being as the creator of writing. In Egypt, this honor was shared by Thoth and Isis, while the ancient Greeks thanked Hermes for their written words. Chinese tradition attributes the invention of writing to Ts'ang Chieh, a minister of the heroic "Yellow Emperor," Huangdi, who, it is said, lived in those misty

*Mel Ziegler, "Sedate Hordes See China Exhibit," *San Francisco Chronicle*, July 15, 1975, p. 3. © Chronicle Publishing Co., 1977.

reaches of time before the Shang dynasty. When men first learned to write, "all spirits cried in agony, as the innermost secrets of nature were thus revealed."*

Tung Tso-pin, a contemporary expert on oracle bones, believes that Neolithic Chinese, occupying Henan and Shandong provinces five thousand years ago, symbolized their thoughts with primitive pictographs. Some of these pictographs were reconstructed in Chapter 2. Writing probably originated in all cultures as a religious instrument, purposely kept complicated and esoteric by priests guarding a sacred mystery, and China was no exception. Writing was too useful politically to remain in the province of religion very long. Inevitably, it became intertwined with politics, and in China, at least, the two have never since been untangled.

After nomadic tribes learned to farm and settled down, tribal chieftains consolidated a power base in cities. The pictographs of their Stone Age ancestors were inadequate for keeping inventories, making contracts, issuing edicts, or even writing love letters. Many more written words were needed, along with a faster style of writing them.

During the legendary Xia dynasty and the Shang dynasty, all types of characters described in Chapter 2— ideographs, hybrids, and phonetic loan words—evolved. Characters were continuously simplified. A royal diviner, laboriously carving a sixteen-stroke character on a turtle carapace, could not be blamed for leaving out a stroke or

---

*Dun J. Li, trans., *The Ageless Chinese* (New York: Charles Scribner's Sons), p. 34.

two, or for sliding lines together. Other writers on silk and bamboo may have followed his simplifications; so might casters of bronze. The earliest examples of Chinese brushwork on perishable silk and bamboo have not survived, although we know they existed. What a pity! They could give us valuable insights into the beginnings of freehand calligraphy. We must be content just to find those ancient characters inscribed in bone and bronze.

Around 1120 B.C., the Shang dynasty gave way to a strife-ridden era historians call Zhou (ca. 1122–249 B.C.), China's Iron Age. Using a maturing written language, increasingly rich in new characters, philosophers and poets lifted their brushes to write great Chinese classics: *The Book of Poetry, The Book of History,* the *I Ching,* or *Book of Changes, The Book of Rites,* and the *Spring and Autumn Annals.* A traveling scholar named Confucius wrote his *Analects* and edited or studied the other classics, which would ever after be associated with his name. During all these hundreds of years, while the empire broke apart and eventually dissolved into fragments of fighting kingdoms,* various styles of writing sprang up and grew side by side. A scribe could choose one of several versions for the same character to express a word, according to his whim or personal style. With sixty-seven ways to write *rén (man),* the situation was getting out of hand.

One of China's most remarkable emperors put a stop

*Historians call the last two centuries of the Zhou dynasty "The Warring States Period."

to this confusion of scripts: Shihuangdi, "The Tiger of Qin." In 221 B.C. he unified the fragments of the Zhou state under a short-lived dynasty called Qin (221–207 B.C.). Order was his byword: He built the Great Wall to fence out wild northern barbarians, and launched a system of canals and irrigation projects to protect farmers from the vagaries of drought and flood.

Shihuangdi was China's first real dictator, and, like later leaders of totalitarian states, he needed and demanded total control of communication. Language was one of his most formidable weapons against opposition. In the West, an early king of Babylon named Hammurabi had his laws engraved on a seven-foot pillar sometime during the eighteenth century before Christ, so his subjects could comprehend and obey his decrees. Shihuangdi, with the same urge for total dominion, promulgated a single code of laws, and, to make sure his subjects would understand it, caused his code to be written in a style known as "small script" or "small seal script." He also declared this script the only legal one, and scholars who wrote in other ways were punished, sometimes with death. Despite his several major contributions, Shihuangdi has not been treated kindly by scholars of subsequent dynasties because of his cruelties.

Table 4.1, marking the milestones in the development of the Chinese language, shows that Shihuangdi's small seal script is the foundation of modern written Chinese characters.

During the time between the Qin dynasty in the second century B.C. and 1919 A.D., the Chinese written

Table 4.1. Milestones in the History of Written Chinese*

Oracle bone	Great seal	Small seal	Official	Model	Running †	Cursive †
馬	馬	馬	馬	馬	馬	馬
中	中	中	中	中	中	中
隹	隹	隹	隹	隹	隹	隹
月	月	月	月	月	月	月
行	行	行	行	行	行	行

*Reprinted from Sau Wing Chan, *Elementary Chinese*, 2nd ed., with the permission of the publishers, Stanford University Press. Copyright © 1951, 1959 by the Board of Trustees of the Leland Stanford Junior University.

†The last two columns are not subsequent developments but freer styles of the "model" or "regular" script still used in China today. More on them in Chapter 7. The meanings of the words are, from top to bottom: *horse, middle, bird, moon,* and *row.*

language developed along lines unparalleled in the West. Since the days of the Caesars, Western nations have used letters of the Roman alphabet to express a mainstream of spoken language that evolved over centuries from classical to Vulgar Latin, from Vulgar Latin to Old French, used by Charlemagne in 842, and finally into modern French, Spanish, and Italian. Roman letters were used to commit the barbarian tongues of northern Europe to writing, and so they are used today for modern German, Dutch, Swedish, and English. Like other phonetic alphabets—Cyrillic (Russian), Hebrew, or Arabic—the Roman system of writing must reflect inevitable changes in a language spoken across hundreds of generations.

Like other spoken tongues, the Chinese spoken language has also altered over the centuries. Yet while the speech of all classes of Chinese mutated as years passed, the written language used by scholars and bureaucrats diverged more and more from the spoken language, and developed at last into a unique literary style that came to be known as *wényán,* or *literary speech.* The word *wényán* can also be used to mean *a body of written classics.*

Western writers test the smoothness and cadence of their prose against the language of articulate speakers. Writers of *wényán* work with a terse, telegraphic prose style quite different from their own way of speaking. Read aloud in the various Chinese dialects, *wényán* sounds more like recitation than everyday conversation.

Wényán differs from common speech in both grammar and vocabulary. The writer of *wényán* uses fewer words to express an idea than does an ordinary speaker, eliminating the extra words that round out a spoken sentence. In its latter days, *wényán* would become somewhat flowery and poetical, like formal Spanish or Victorian poetry, but the best *wényán* is marked by brevity when compared to spoken Chinese. *Wényán* also developed a separate vocabulary of literary words, used only for writing, and never heard in speech. For example, *wényán* uses different characters to represent *you* and *I.*

To add to this complexity, *wényán* is studded with literary, mythical, and historical allusions. It is not really possible to read and understand just one piece of *wényán.* *Wényán* requires well-educated readers, well versed in history, literature, philosophy, and the arts.

It is difficult to convey an impression of *wényán* in

Common
speech

我 你
wǒ   *nǐ*
(I)   (you)

Wényán

余 汝
yū   *rū*
(I)   (you)

English translation, for English has no purely literary language, nor do neighboring branches on the Indo-European linguistic tree. The following quote from the Tudor writer Edward Hall conveys something of the flavor of *wényán* to the modern reader of English:

> Oblivion, the cankered enemy to fame and renown, the sucking serpent of ancient memory, the deadly dart to the glory of princes, and the defacer of all conquests and notable acts, so much bare rule in the first and second age of the world that nothing was set out to men's knowledge, either how the world was made, either how man and beasts were created, or how the world was destroyed by water till father Moses had, by divine inspiration in the third age, invented letters, the treasure of memory, and set forth five notable books to the great comfort of all people living at this day. Likewise Mercury in Egypt invented letters and writing, which Cadmus after brought into Greece. So every nation was desirous to enhance Lady Fame and to suppress that deadly beast Oblivion.*

Probably no subject of Henry VIII's son, the boy king Edward VI, to whom this piece was dedicated, spoke this way on the streets of London or Canterbury, and the references to Mercury and Cadmus might have puzzled many. Hall's diction is literary, and he writes for a reader thoroughly grounded in Greek and Roman chronicles and myths, as well as in Biblical matters and English history.

The astute reader and polished writer of *wényán* spent a lifetime cultivating his writing skill and savoring the

*Hebel, Hudson, Johnson, Green, and Hoopes, eds., *Tudor Poetry and Prose*, © 1953, p. 587. Reprinted by permission of Prentice-Hall, Inc., Englewood Cliffs, N.J.

vast banquet of Chinese classics. In the sixth century A.D., while Europe plunged into the depths of the Dark Ages, civil-service examinations, testing skill in composition and calligraphy, were introduced in China. In theory, at least, any young man, even a despised butcher's son, could attain a powerful government post through mastery of *wényán* and extensive study of Chinese philosophy, history, and poetry.

Civil-service examinations, part of China's political and cultural life for twelve centuries, created a powerful intelligentsia whose skills in composition, calligraphy, and administration were valued even above the military genius of brilliant generals. Once language had been an esoteric secret of priests. Now scholar-bureaucrats maintained their position at the peak of society by keeping written language difficult and exclusive. Obviously, only wealthy young men, or those few poor ones supported by the toil of their relatives, could afford the years of study required to gain proficiency in *wényán*, their passport to political power.

Meanwhile, how did illiterate peasants and the urban poor use the written word? They could read a few characters, sometimes simplified versions of the ones used by the educated minority, enough to transact business and find wineshops. Everybody needs stories or songs, even coolies and sedan chair bearers. The epigrammatic poetry of the intellectuals was out of their reach, but traveling storytellers, often blind, carried vast collections of folktales and poetry in their heads. During the Song dynasty (960– 1279 A.D.), some of these popular stories, poems, and historical tales were written down by people of education in a vernacular style that reproduced everyday language.

Authors of these collections usually remained anonymous rather than arouse the contempt of the intellectual establishment, which despised any writing that mirrored common speech. Commoners loved the collections, in spite of the opinions of their betters, and the popularity of these vernacular tales gave impetus to a newly burgeoning printing industry.

When the Song dynasty, that pinnacle of refined culture, toppled before the cataclysmic invasion of barbarian Mongol tribes, the Han Chinese found themselves ruled by the Yuan dynasty (1279–1368 A.D.). Its founder, the Mongol emperor Kublai Khan, grandson of Genghis Khan, was celebrated in Europe by the writings of Marco Polo, who visited his court.

The Yuan dynasty, illiterate though its Mongol leaders were, managed one major cultural achievement: musical drama, a widely popular entertainment combining songs in *wényán* or "semi-*wényán*" with dialogue inspired by common speech, even by street slang. These dramas were written down, adding their lively conversations and lyrics to the accumulating body of vernacular literature.

Chinese authors writing during the Yuan dynasty used simple, nonliterary Chinese for two enormously popular novels: *The Three Kingdoms,* a historic tale of the third century A.D., and *The Marsh Heroes* (or *The Water Margin*), based on traditional stories about a band of outlaws, who, like Robin Hood and his Merry Men, robbed the rich and gave to the poor. Time has not diminished the widespread love Chinese of all classes feel for these books; they are still being sold in Chinese-language bookstores around the world, and in 1975, *The Marsh Heroes* became a symbol of conflict between opposing factions in the government of the People's Republic of China.

During China's last two imperial dynasties, Ming (1368–1644 A.D.) and Qing (1644–1912 A.D.), *The Three Kingdoms* and *The Marsh Heroes* were followed by a deluge of novels written in vernacular, some with a style as hackneyed and characterizations as stereotyped as the Horatio Alger or Elsie Dinsmore books of nineteenth-century America. Others, significantly *The Dream of the Red Chamber*, a sentimental romance, had great literary merit. Contemporary masters of *wényán*, involved in rigidly formalized poetry and intricate philosophical debates, looked down their aristocratic noses at these popular novels. Like Shaker furniture, Mexican folk art, Japanese prints, and so many other popular arts scorned by contemporary arbiters of good taste, it took later generations of Chinese, and even foreigners, to appreciate the artistic merit of these novels. Now they are ranked with the greatest pieces of world literature. Until recently, they were not available to Chinese on the Mainland, for they are hardly suitable as revolutionary inspiration.

Our history of Chinese writing has come full circle, back to the last despairing years of the nineteenth century.

As one military and economic debacle followed another, succeeding generations were forced to question ancient Chinese wisdom and learn more about Western ideas. The Qing dynasty, established in 1644 by Manchurian foreigners from the north, had totally embraced the culture of the conquered Han people. *Wényán* had become more deeply entrenched as centuries passed. Even newspapers were printed in the difficult literary style. In 1912, Republicans led by Sun Yat-sen rid China of a decrepit imperial rule and established a government modeled after Western democracies, while the year 1919 saw the most important revolution in Chinese writing since the Tiger of Qin decreed the use of small seal script more than two thousand years ago.

In the first years of the twentieth century, a smoldering Chinese nationalism, kindled by newspaper accounts of diplomatic concessions to Japan and the West, burst into flame. On May 4, 1919, news reached Beijing that Chinese diplomats attending the Paris Peace Conference ending the First World War had not been able to wrest Shandong from Japanese hands. Tens of thousands of students took to the streets in protest: the May Fourth Movement began, and China was never the same again.

Hu Shih, an American-educated professor at Beijing University, spearheaded an intellectual break with the past emanating from the May Fourth Movement, later called the "Chinese Renaissance." Recognizing that China's glimmering dreams of democracy could only be realized with literate masses, Hu had for years been urging his ivory pagoda compatriots to abandon *wényán* and write as they spoke, in *bái huà*, or *plain speech*, so that most Chinese could easily read what they wrote.

bái
(plain)

huà
(speech)

The May Fourth demonstrators took up Hu Shih's cause, demanding the abolition of *wényán*. Overnight, it happened. Newspapers and magazines were soon printed in *bái huà*. School texts were rewritten in *bái huà*. University students shocked their parents and tutors by using *bái huà* in the letters they wrote home.

The hopes of Sun Yat-sen, Hu Shih, and the rest of that early generation of revolutionaries for a republican China were doomed in the end by the overpopulation, starvation, and banditry that engulfed their people. The 1937 Japanese invasion was republican China's final blow. Chiang Kai-shek, Sun Yat-sen's successor, was pushed back to Chongqing by the Japanese, then driven from the Chinese Mainland in 1949 by the Communists. Hu Shih followed Chiang to Chongqing and from there to Taiwan, where he died. His torch of language reform, a light to guide the Chinese masses out of illiterate darkness, sputtered but did not go out, for it was plucked from flood-rubble by a man Hu Shih had probably forgotten, a gangly adolescent from the boondocks who had attended Hu Shih's lectures at Beijing University while living on a meager salary earned by working in the university library. This man's name was Mao Zedong.

Mao had his dreams too, dreams of restoring China to her historic place, strong and independent, a giant among nations. He pursued his dreams with a fervor Americans should recognize, for the same single-minded idealism impelled the Pilgrim Fathers to leave their comfortable homes in the Old World and cross an unknown ocean to a wild new continent, where they established a Puritan religious state. Their ideology was the Word of God, which they believed every soul must be able to read for himself in the Bible. Like them, Mao realized that universal literacy was the cornerstone of his new society. Unless they could all read, the Chinese people had no hope of casting off the ancient bonds of class, of learning technical skills, or even of feeding or housing themselves properly.

It is no coincidence that *wényán*'s two-millennium supremacy ended just nine years after the overthrow of a four-thousand-year-old imperial government. *Wényán*, unique among written languages for refined complexity, was ideally suited to a country ruled by an elite minority and supported by peasants, craftsmen, and artisans whose skills were acquired through lore, not book learning. The dismantling of the old society, begun by Sun Yat-sen's government, was continued relentlessly by leaders of the People's Republic of China. Scientists, engineers, and doctors had to be trained, and trained quickly. Even Hu Shih's vernacular Chinese took too much time to learn, and time is money in a technologically developing country.

As soon as they could begin to pick up the pieces of their war-broken nation, Communist Chinese leaders mounted a three-part campaign against illiteracy. Their first tactic was to establish a standard list of simplified characters. Simplified versions of extremely complicated characters had been used since the Song dynasty by semi-literates as well as writers of vernacular novels. Usually, characters are simplified by reducing the number of strokes and borrowing abbreviations frequently used by generations of literate Chinese for writing notes and letters. Table 4.2 lists some examples of simplified characters used today in the People's Republic of China. The established list of simplified characters has never been considered final, but all Mainland books, magazines, and newspapers are now printed in the new characters. Children learn them in school, then shift without much difficulty to the complex characters found in older books.

Having to learn a symbol for every word, even a simplified symbol, is, as noted before, a cumbersome and time-consuming business. Language reformers in the People's Republic for the past twenty years have been replacing ideographs with a phonetic alphabet, but before they remove the only language which ties all China together—*written* Chinese—they must have all

Table 4.2. Some Simplified Characters*

Original character	Simplified character	Pīnyīn	Meaning
國 (11)	国 (7)	guó	country, nation
廠 (15)	厂 (2)	chǎng	factory
門 (7)	门 (3)	mén	door
會 (13)	会 (6)	huì	meeting, can
馬 (10)	马 (3)	mǎ	horse
幾 (11)	几 (2)	jǐ	several

*The number in parentheses indicates the number of strokes.

China *speaking* the same dialect. This does not necessarily mean that the dialects described in Chapter 1 must be abolished, just that one dialect would be learned by all Chinese, if not as a first language, then as a second. The natural choice for a universal dialect is the pure Beijing dialect known in the West as Mandarin but called *pǔtōnghuà*, or *common language*, on the Mainland today. This dialect is also used by the government of the Republic of China on Taiwan, who give it another name, *guó yǔ*, or *national speech*. Starting in the autumn of 1956, official policy has called for the gradual ascendancy of *pǔtōnghuà*, using official speeches, radio programs, and schools as vehicles for spreading the word.

There is a built-in contradiction between the need to implement *pǔtōnghuà* as a national dialect and Mao's belief that all changes in society should spring up from the people, not flow down from above. The Chairman himself did not speak perfect *pǔtōnghuà*, and took pride in the individuality of his provincial Hunan accent. Once China proclaimed its dedication to preserving regional dialects. Now the widespread use of computers favors *pǔtōnghuà*, for reasons we shall explain.

Once a standard spoken dialect is established, it can be written in phonetic symbols. A government committee on language reform, working from 1955 to 1956, chose the Roman alphabet for a new phonetic rendering of spoken Chinese, called *Pīnyīn*, which was described in Chapter 2. Today, *Pīnyīn* is taught as a bridge to Chinese characters for illiterate adults and children beginning school. When they complete primary school, children should be able to read their *pǔtōnghuà* both in *Pīnyīn* Romanization and in 2,800 to 3,000 simplified characters. In middle school, skill in writing Chinese characters is refined and content of reading is emphasized.

An interesting sidelight on the spread of literacy in China is the official government policy toward non-Han minority languages, like Uigur, Kazakh, Mongol, and Tibetan. Linguists from Chinese universities have established a system of Romanization for tongues previously written with complex symbols, or never written down at all. While Han Chinese are encouraged to speak *pǔtōnghuà*, non-Han minorities are encouraged to nurture their native language and culture. Because the Mainland government wants these people to read, it provides newspapers, books, magazines, and official propaganda in all minority languages.

The Communist Revolution has brought many new words to the Chinese language. In their efforts to remove the class system from every fiber of Chinese society, the Communists have used a technique called *gīngsuàn doùzhēng. Gīngsuàn* is a compound the dictionary translates as *liquidate,* in the sense of *get rid of old debts.* Here it means recounting one's past history in great detail. *Doùzhēng* is *struggle.* The four words together describe what a former capitalist, landowner, banker, or Nationalist government official had to do to be accepted by the people he once exploited; stand on a public stage, recount his past misdeeds, and listen to former peasants, workers, or servants denounce him. This public trial, a most terrifying and devastating experience for anyone who has gone through the process, is called *self-criticism*, *zì wǒ pī píng (I me criticize)*.

The year 1958 saw the Great Leap Forward, *Dà Yuè Jìn*, and 1966 brought the Great Proletarian *(wù chǎn jiē jí, or people with no property)* Cultural Revolution *(wèn huà dà gé mìng*, or *culture large revolution)*—a period of civil strife born in the idea that a revolution must renew itself in every generation. The *Hóng Wèi Bīng, Red Guards*, implemented the renewed revolution, and set out to destroy all reactionaries, or *fǎn dòng pài*, a phrase that literally translates as *turn over move group* and means *movement to turn against*.

When a totalitarian government wants to shape the thoughts of a widespread, diverse population, political slogans are essential. The Chinese Communist government has coined hundreds of political slogans. Mao was a master at writing slogans; his Little Red Book, *The Sayings of Chairman Mao*, is known throughout the world. When workers were assigned to a flood control project on the Wei He, a river that had for centuries destroyed lives and property with its floods, they labored under a banner that read, *"Yī dìng yào bǎ Wei He zhì hǎo,"* *"We must control Wei He!"* Mao had said it; the workers revered him; and so the saying inspired them to do their best, and build a dam that tamed the river at last.

Focusing admiration on a leader is an easy way to unite a people. Mao was the object of mass devotion, and of him people would say, *"Mao zhǔ xí wàn suì!,"* *"Long live Chairman Mao."* *Wàn suì* means literally *ten thousand years* and was once an honorific attached to the emperor. One of China's best-known slogans is the Marxist phrase

"Unite, Workers of the World!," or *"Shì jiè gōng rén dà tuán jié."* Another phrase heard often on the Mainland was *"Wéi rén mín fú wù," "Serve the people."* Art must serve the people; literature must serve the people; music must serve the people; research must serve the people. An artist, poet, musician, or scientist, like a medieval artisan working for the glory of God, often becomes an anonymous team member. Anyone ambitious for individual glory does not serve the people and is liable to need political reeducation.

Those who delight in the uses of the past may want to know what has happened to *wényán*. Enclaves of scholars and poets in Taiwan and other overseas Chinese communities still read and write in the old way. Middle school students in the People's Republic are taught to read *wényán* through textbooks of selected readings, but are not asked to compose or to read the original classics in their entirety, for reasons that are as much political as educational. The classics were literature for the elite; they do not serve the people, and so are not considered proper reading material for future builders of an egalitarian state. Yet, as modern archaeology illuminates larger and larger swaths of China's splendid past, interest in classical language grows, for *wényán* is an important link with four thousand years of noble achievement in arts and literature.

Five

DOMESTIC
CHINESE

Chinese at home.

The phrase evokes a picture of a vocal family group, varying in age from eighty to five, gathered around the dinner table, their conversation punctuated with laughter and perfectly timed swoops of their chopsticks into serving platters filled with savory food. In prewar China, a servant would stand in the background, poised to fill a rice bowl or remove an empty serving plate.

To the Chinese, the best kind of family contains five generations living under one roof. Traditionally, the oldest male takes charge of all the family's affairs. His wife, whose marriage was arranged and who was not supposed to have seen her husband until the wedding day, rules the household with a firm hand. Chinese women do not dread middle age; for them it ends years of total subservience and brings long deferred power over the events of their everyday lives.* Sons and grandsons bring their wives home to live, and grandsons and great-grandsons are happily welcomed as insurance that the family will continue forever.

This chapter is devoted to "domestic Chinese," the words and phrases used between family members and friends. We discuss the diversity of names for people and throw in a few names for places as well. We will select a few interesting examples from the vocabulary of food and cooking, look at the everyday symbolism of colors, and dip into the ample store of proverbial wisdom a Chinese matriarch carries about in her head.

Everyone is rejoicing: parents and grandparents, uncles and aunts, brothers and sisters, for the newborn baby is a boy.

What will his name be?

The choice is most important; it cannot be left to the whims of young parents, so Chinese tradition gives paternal grandparents the responsibility for selecting a name. They can take their time about it, and sometimes several months go by before the most auspicious name is chosen.

The new baby is born with a family name or surname, Ma (yes, it means *horse*) from his father's side. Chinese

---

*In the People's Republic today, particularly in the cities, sexual equality prevails. One of the major accomplishments of the Mainland government was the emancipation of women.

surnames are spoken and written first, before any other name or title. Sometimes they have a meaning, but never the occupational identifications found in the English surnames Smith, or *blacksmith*, Cooper, or *barrelmaker*, Chapman, or *peddler*. A few Chinese family names with other meanings are Mi, or *rice*, Jin, or *gold*, and Tian, or *field*, as well as homonyms for color like Huáng, *yellow*, or Bái, *white*.

Long isolated from other cultures, and given to assimilating both immigrants and conquerors, the Middle Kingdom has a limited supply of one-syllable surnames, plus a few two-syllable surnames. This nation of 1.2 billion people, give or take one hundred million (not counting overseas Chinese), draws from a pool of approximately four hundred family names, or one name for every two million people, assuming equal distribution. Actually, some surnames are much more common than others.

To complicate matters, some surnames belong to the same group of homonyms and sound alike, although they are written differently. Consider the near homonyms Wang (王) and Huang (黃) and the homonyms Chang (Zhang in *Pīnyīn*), which is either 張 or 章. How does a person avoid confusion when speaking in conversation or over the telephone? The Huangs and Wangs have the least trouble. One of them may say, "My name is the three-stroke Wang," referring to the 三 in 王. The other would say, "My name is the same as the color," because 黃 is the character for *yellow*. The Changs encounter more difficulty. Both characters for *Chang* have the same number of strokes (11), so that characteristic cannot be used to distinguish them. Fortunately, the radicals in both names are words themselves, so Mr. Chang can say, "My name is *gōng* (弓) *cháng* (長) Chang (張)," or "My name is *lì* (立) *zǎo* (早) Chang (章)" to make his correct name clear.

Because of the variant dialects, the same written surname may be pronounced differently, according to the dialect of one's home province. The name Huang (黃) is a case in point. As mentioned earlier, *Huang* is the *Pīnyīn* Romanization that follows the Mandarin pronunciation of *yellow*. The Cantonese, however, pronounce the same character *Wong*. In fact, in Cantonese 黃 and 王 have exactly the same sound.

In this chapter, as in the rest of the book, we have used commonly accepted spelling for Chinese surnames, unless there was a particular reason for using *Pīnyīn* Romanization. Many Romanizations for Chinese surnames found in the United States happen to follow *Pīnyīn*, omitting the accent marks. Western spelling of Chinese surnames is extremely haphazard, as our name shows. The character is a modifier for sheets of paper, paintings, tables, and other flat objects. Its *Pīnyīn* Romanization is *Zhang*, but it is more commonly spelled *Chang*. One obvious advantage is that Chang is usually served long before Zhang.

Library cataloguers, people who care about consistency, establish one spelling for each surname character and stick to it, whether it agrees with the author's own spelling or not. That way, all Chinese books or the English translations of Chinese books by people of the

same surname are grouped together in the library catalogue, just as in the case of Western authors.

Cai

To illustrate the problems various pronunciations can
cause, consider the married woman from Beijing who
pronounced her name in perfect Mandarin, *Tsai (Cài* in
Pīnyīn). She had great difficulty explaining to American
immigration officials that she was, indeed, related to a
family of brothers-in-law named Choy, even though she
had a "different" name. Her brothers-in-law had all immi-
grated from Guangzhou and used the Cantonese pronunciation of the character in the margin, which, incidentally,
is a homonym for *vegetable* or *cooked dish.*

Speaking of married women, until the mid-1960s, an
American woman always discarded her own name when
she married, unless she had a previously established pro-
fessional or artistic reputation. Once married, Mary Margaret Reilly would ever after be known as Mrs. Otto
Schmidt, or, to her friends, Mary Schmidt. The Chinese
are not so rigid about this convention. A Chinese woman
frequently retains her maiden names after marriage, for
both social and legal purposes. She may also use her own
name and her husband's name together, as European
women sometimes do.

If a Chinese woman with the surname Zhou and the
given name Qing-mei marries a man named Feng with
a given name De-ming, she is either called Feng *Tàitài,*
Mrs. Feng, by those who address her formally, or Zhou
Qing-mei by those who may use her given name. She
never attaches her own given name to her husband's, nor
does she ever go by her husband's given name, as does

that irrepressibly Irish Mrs. Otto Schmidt.

The most common Chinese surname is Li (often spelled *Lee*). An old story accounts for its popularity. Although ancient emperors were supposed to cherish their people as children, they could not tolerate a subject who bore the imperial name. If an Emperor Bái came to the throne, all the Báis would quickly change names to avoid harassment or even death. When the will of heaven brought good Emperor Li Shi-min to the throne during the Tang dynasty (618–906 A.D.), he extended his benevolence even to the sharing of names. He did not persecute people named Li, in fact, he encouraged his "children" to take Li as a surname.

Until recently, rural villages might be populated by three or four thousand people with the same surname— Chen, perhaps, or Wong in Guangdong Province—of whom many, but not all, were related. Girls from such villages would have to leave their home towns to marry, as Chinese tradition frowns upon a marriage between two people with the same surname, even if the two do not belong to the same family. As they say in China about people named alike, "Five hundred years ago, we were all of the same family." Another Chinese proverb goes: "Children with parents of the same surname will have much misfortune." Folk wisdom understood enough genetics to recognize the ill effects of inbreeding. Today only a few Chinese would be deterred from the marriage of their choice by this old-fashioned taboo.

Folk wisdom did not recognize the female genetic legacy, though, because this antique prohibition applied only to the male line. First cousins on the mother's side, who would not have the same surname, could marry without social disapproval.

周
Zhou

恩
en
(thanksgiving)

來
lai
(come)

Back in the Ma family nursery, a proud grandfather is considering what two-syllable given name will follow his grandson's surname. Grandfather Ma has an exceptionally wide range of choice, since he does not select a name from a standard list as Westerners do. Sometimes two characters are picked purely for their sound; sometimes for their meaning. Zhou En-lai, the first premier of the People's Republic of China, had a name with a meaning: *Thanksgiving Comes.*

Boys are often given names representing a hoped-for destiny or character trait, like *Modest and Wise.* Daughters get feminine, poetic names of lesser significance — *Lotus*, for example, or *Precious Jade.* A firstborn girl could be named *Hope for a Little Brother.* Families blessed with many children commonly use the same second syllable in each boy's given name, varying only the first syllable. This second syllable corresponds to the Western middle name, as we can see if we reverse a Chinese name, which is frequently done to avoid confusion when Chinese travel abroad. Zhou En-lai would be En-lai Zhou, making Lai the middle name. A group of boys with the same surname and second syllable in their given names would be immediately recognized as brothers.

The Western custom of naming a boy after his father — John T. Williams, Jr., for example — is unheard of in China, where it is considered highly disrespectful for the son to have the same name as his father — not to mention his grandfather, as in John T. Williams III! In fact, ancient calligraphers transcribing a manuscript would avoid using characters for the names of their ancestors or even of the reigning emperor.

Grandfather Ma has decided. His little grandson shall be called Ma Wu-jiang, or *Boundless Future*, by all his Chinese-speaking friends and relations. For a family living in, say, Chengdu, on the Chinese Mainland, this would be the end of naming. Overseas Chinese frequently add a local name. If Ma Wu-jiang was born in San Francisco, he would probably grow up hearing his grandfather call "Wu-jiang!" while his playmates yelled for "Willy!"

馬
Ma

無
wu
(no)

疆
jiang
(boundary)

A Chinese student or emigrant without a Western name will surely take one when he settles abroad. Western co-workers and friends have trouble remembering and pronouncing Chinese given names. His new name may be close to the old one in sound, as Wang Da-wei becomes David Wang. Or fresh-off-the-boat Chinese may christen themselves with any name they like, to the envy and amazement of their friends.

Little Wu-jiang, the sixth child of the Ma family, learns how to address his five brothers and sisters as soon as he is able to talk. He will not use given names; Chinese families rarely do at home. No Chinese child would ever call his father and mother by their given names; that is the height of disrespect. Ma Wu-jiang's siblings were born in this order: male, male, female, male, female. All five younger children call the eldest *Big Brother*. The next born is *Two Brother*. The last three children refer to the oldest girl as *Big Sister*. The third boy is called *Three Brother*, the younger girl *Two Sister*, and everyone speaks of Ma Wu-jiang as *Four Brother*.

Chinese indicates family relationships with great precision, as the following examples will show. There are two words for *brother: gēgē, older brother*, and *dìdì, younger brother*. Similarly, *sister* translates as *jiějiě, older sister*, or *mèimèi, younger sister*. When Ma Wu-jiang speaks of *Two Sister*, he says *èrjiě*, making it clear that the Mas' second daughter is his older sister. The eldest brother would call the same sister *èrmèi*.

gē
(older
brother)

dì
(younger
brother)

jiě
(older
sister)

mèi
(younger
sister)

fù   *mǔ*
(father)   (mother)

Mandarin-speaking babies call their father *Bàbà* and their mothers *Māmā*, equivalent to *Daddie* and *Mommie* in English. When they grow older, they may switch to the more respectful terms *Fùqìng* and *Mǔqìng*. As for the rest of the family, the numbering system extends to uncles and aunts, preceding words indicating the maternal or paternal side and, sometimes, uncle's or aunt's age in relation to the parent. Father's second sister would be *èrgūmā, two father's sister*. When brothers and sisters marry, there are special words meaning *older sister's husband, younger sister's husband, older brother's wife*, or *younger brother's wife*. Cousins, nieces, and nephews are also named according to their exact genealogical place on the family tree.

When Ma Wu-jiang speaks of his grandparents, he uses four words. *Grandmother* is either *zǔmǔ, father's mother*, or *wàipó, mother's mother*. *Grandfather* translates as *zǔfù, father's father*, or *wàigōng, mother's father*. The first word in compounds denoting maternal grandparents is *wài*, or *outside*. Because a Chinese woman left her own home to live with her husband's family, her children would naturally think of her parents as outside people, outside the walls that enclosed them with their paternal grandparents. The specific nomenclature for Chinese family names extends even to the dead — for example, the word *bĭ* means *my deceased mother*, but it is used only in writing, never in speaking. The same rule applies to *kăo*, *my deceased father*.

The Chinese have a neat solution for a naming problem that stumps Americans: What should a small child call his parents' close friends? Once, proper American children were trained to call a woman Mother saw every day "Mrs. Gertmanian," even though Mother called her "Nancy," and the infant tongue might stumble over this longer name. It is easier for the child to enjoy a first-name relationship with his parents' friends, but this violates the sensibilities of decorous traditionalists. Ma Wu-jiang will call adults he meets infrequently "Mr. Chen," or "Mrs. Lu," but close adult friends are addressed by their first names, followed by a word that best translates as "Uncle" or "Auntie," and adds just the right degree of respect to the comfortable first name.

When Ma Wu-jiang goes to school, his playmates will christen him all over again with a nickname, one he may keep all his life. Chinese nicknames often relate to age. Ma Wu-jiang may call his younger friend "Small Li," while Li rejoins with "Old Ma." Once a pattern is established, it will be maintained by all their friends, younger and older alike.

The Chinese are also fond of nicknames based on physical characteristics. Though a nickname may be baldly descriptive, usually no malice is intended. A Cantonese distinguished by his height might be dubbed "Tallman," a tall Shanghainese, "Longshanks." Portly men are called "Tubby" and thin men "Skinny" to their faces, but only by equals or superiors. Never would a worker call his boss by a nickname, nor a son his father.

Chinese also has its share of honorifics. Teachers and men of learning were traditionally honored in China with the title *Xiānshēng*, literally *born first*, which has always meant *teacher* and is now translated as *Mr.* A student calls his teachers, both male and female, *Huang Xiānshēng* or *Zhāng Xiānshēng*. He also uses *Xiānshēng* for adult males an English-speaking child would call "Mr. Abbott" or "Mr. Kerr." Married women were always called *Tàitài* or *Fūrén* by people who wished to show respect, like shopkeepers and servants, but *lǎo pó, old lady*, or *jiàn nèi, humble inside woman*, by their husbands. The first appellation *(lǎo pó)* is respectfully familiar, the second *(jiàn nèi)* again reflects the male dominance in old Chinese society. When speaking to their spouses or referring to them in their presence, Chinese women use *zhàng fū*, or *husband.* Husbands not near the site of conversation are called *wài zǐ*, or *outside person.*

Parents or respected elders are honored with special forms of the pronouns *you, he,* and *she* shown in the margin. The top part of each word is the same as the ordinary version, but the radical for *heart* added below denotes respect.

你
心
nín
(you)

他
心
tān
(he)

The emperor was often designated the *Son of Heaven*, and sometimes *wàn suì*, or *ten thousand years*, an extravagantly respectful term implying longevity accompanied by wisdom. Courtiers, those Mandarin scholar-bureaucrats, were deferentially titled *Big Man (Dà Rén)* by a humble subject, who then spoke of himself as *Xiǎo Rén* —*Small Person.* A servant might address his master as *Lǎo Yé, Old Grandfather*, which sounds more formal in Chinese than it does in English.

Terms of respect for a superior by his inferior were eliminated on the Mainland after 1949 as part of the effort to establish a classless society. *Tóngzhì*, or *comrade*, is the only word that comes after a surname in the People's Republic of China these days. Degrading terms have also been abolished, along with degrading jobs like pulling a rickshaw or selling one's sexual services. *Coolie* is now *gōng rén*, or *factory worker.* Husbands and wives now call each other *àiren*, or *lover*, a proper word on the Mainland since 1949. *Àiren* was never used in family conversation before then, certainly never to describe a wife! Even today, the word makes conservative overseas Chinese blush.

同
tóng
(same)

志
zhì
(purpose)

Chinese is rich in ways to name but poor in ways to greet. There is no exact equivalent for *hello* in Chinese. When two people meet for the first time in the morning, they say *Zǎo*, literally *early*, meaning *good morning.* Yet there are no analogous words for afternoon and evening. During these periods, an appropriate greeting might be *How are you? (Nǐ hǎo ma?)* Two people parting at night might say *Wǎn ān, peaceful night. Goodbye* is *Zài jiàn*, *again see,* or *Míng tiān jiàn, tomorrow see.*

The merriest greetings come on the Chinese New Year when *Gōng xǐ fā cái (Congratulations and may you make a fortune)* is heard in every street and house. Other traditional greetings are *Duō shēng guì zǐ, Hope you will have many distinguished sons,* and *Chū rù píng àn, May you be safe on all your trips.* Still another good wish is *Wàn shì rú yì,* literally *May ten thousand things come your way,* or *May all your dreams come true.*

A Chinese may open a telephone conversation with, *Nǐ shì shéi,* or *Who are you?*—hostile in English, but acceptable in Chinese. When Mr. Shi is introduced to Mr. Liang, Mr. Shi does not say, *How do you do?* (This English expression sounds very strange to foreigners.) Instead he says, *Liang Xiānshēng, nǐ hǎo,* or *Mr. Liang, you well?*

Chinese speakers use vivid similes for expressing affection and contempt. A beloved only daughter is a *pearl on the palm,* while the son of traditional parents would be called, with modest tenderness, *my little dog.* A doting mother may say to her son, *"You are my heart-liver treasure."*

Someone who stares rudely might be taunted, *What's the matter, don't you know your father?,* imputing loose morals to the starer's mother. Another very insulting epithet, to the Chinese, is *turtle* because it hides its head inside its shell. Worse still is being called *son of a turtle.* A bad fellow is called a *bad egg* or *mixed egg. Pig* does not express total contempt, as it does in Romance languages, but is used in Chinese to indicate laziness or obesity. The word *animal* is applied to people with the same connotation as in English. Someone despicable is said to be *gǒu niáng yǎng de, born of a dog's mother,* or as Americans put it, *son of a bitch.*

Surprisingly, the term *flower embroidered pillow* is an insult, too, for it implies that a person looks pretty as an embroidered pillow on the outside, but has inside him, like the pillows of old, nothing but straw. Along this same line, someone admired for beauty alone is a *huā píng,* or *flower vase.*

The Chinese speak of foreigners, especially Caucasians, as *yáng guǐ zǐ (ocean devil),* meaning a devil from across the ocean, or *foreign devil.* A more polite term is *wài guó rén,* or *outside country person,* which Chinese are more likely to use with foreigners who understand Chinese.

Owing to the purity of the language, the etymology of Chinese place names is obvious to its speakers. While Americans must consult a dictionary to know that *Massachusetts* is derived from an Indian word meaning *At the Big Hill,* a Chinese speaking the word *Beijing* (Peking) knows he is saying *Northern Capital. Nanjing* (Nanking), about five hundred miles to the south, means *Southern Capital.* The largest city in China, a commercial port named Shanghai, gave English the verb *shanghaied,* or abducted for service aboard a ship. It means in Chinese *On Top of the Sea. Yunnan,* the name of a province across the border from Burma and Indochina, where rains are heavy, means *Clouds in the South.* The agriculturally rich province of Sichuan, known for its spicy food, is matter-of-factly termed *Four Rivers.* Two other prosaic place names are Manchuria, or *Northeast,* and Sinkiang (*Xinjiang* in *Pīnyīn*), or *New Boundary.* Other provinces have more poetic names, like Heilongjiang, *Black Dragon River;* Chilin, *Magic Forest;* Liaoning, *Distant Peace;* Anhui, *Peaceful Honor.*

Recent participants in the frenetic commercial activity of Hong Kong may find its derivation from the Chinese *Fragrant Harbor* inappropriate. Kowloon, the mainland adjunct to Hong Kong, means *Nine Dragons.*

During the nineteenth century, Yankee clipper ships sailed past Kowloon up the Pearl River to a city once known to the West as Canton, now spelled *Guangzhou* in *Pīnyīn,* bringing ginseng roots, otter furs, and cash to trade for tea and silk. In 1848 they brought a golden dream as well, a dream that caused wretched coolies to leave their life of hopeless toil in civilized China to make their fortunes in the land of the barbarians. They indentured themselves by the boatload to reach the gold fields of California, called by Cantonese to this day the *Mountain of Gold.* San Francisco, the first city they reached, is the *Old Mountain of Gold.* For most immigrants, the new country turned out to be a mountain of laundry, but that is another story.

The *yáng guǐ zǐ* who lived on the Mountain of Gold soon learned that the small newcomers were good launderers and better cooks. Ever since then, Americans have known more about Chinese cooking than any other aspect of Chinese culture. Until the 1960s, most Americans knew only the Cantonese style of cooking, with its fried rice, egg roll, and sweet and sour pork, for that was most easily available to them. In the last twenty years,

Chinese restaurants serving specialties of Sichuan, Shanghai, Hunan, Harbin, and Beijing have opened in most large cities, giving Americans a chance to taste a broad range of Chinese regional cooking.

Except in the northernmost provinces, the staple food, the "bread" of China, is rice. The Chinese have two different words for *rice*. *Mǐ* means uncooked rice, while *fàn* is cooked rice and can be taken in the broad sense to mean any cooked grain. At mealtimes, each diner has a bowl of rice to serve as a base for *cài*, the diced bits of meat and vegetables cooked and served in their own sauce on platters set out upon the middle of the table. Chinese snacks are small portions of food, often dumplings or meatballs, served without rice. These are called *diǎn xīn* (*dim sum* in Cantonese), which means, literally, *a dot on the heart.*

米
mǐ
(uncooked rice)

飯
fàn
(cooked rice)

Sichuanese dishes are often strongly laced with red peppers. The Chinese describe this highly spiced food with the word *là*. English has no exact equivalent but must borrow the word *hot* to describe food that makes the uninitiated beg for water.

Like Western hot cross buns, many Chinese foods carry a traditional symbolism that marks special occasions. The egg, *dàn* in Chinese, is an emblem of life in the East as it is in the West. Although, as we mentioned earlier, *bad egg (huài dàn)* describes a foul fellow, a red egg has quite a different meaning. When little Ma Wujiang is one month old, the proud family gives a party to celebrate the occasion. Red eggs are always served at an infant boy's one-month party.

While we are speaking of eggs, we should mention a

salty egg, discolored from the inside by age and preserving medium. The Chinese consider this greenish-black *pí dàn*, or *skin egg*, a delicacy. Americans call *pí dàn thousand-year-old eggs* (an inexplicable name, because the eggs are no more than three months old) and relish them as little as another Chinese delicacy, silkworm grubs.

When the Chinese celebrate a birthday, they serve noodles instead of birthday cake, for the long, stringy shape suggests long life. These special noodles are called *cháng shòu miàn*, or *longevity noodles*.

The lunar New Year, highest feast of all on the Chinese calendar, is traditionally a three-day orgy of eating and gambling. Drop-in guests are offered trays of tasty candies, among them lotus seeds, *lián zǐ*. Because the first word is a homonym for *to add* or *to follow by*, and the second means *sons*, lotus seeds represent the host's wish that his guests will have consecutive distinguished sons.

One last example of a symbolic Chinese food is the moon cake, *yuè bǐng*, which recalls an event from traditional history. Genghis Khan's Mongolian hordes swept over civilized China, clearing a path for Kublai Khan, who established the Yuan dynasty (1279–1368 A.D.). The Yuan dynasty lasted only eighty-nine years, more than long enough for the Han Chinese, who regarded their Mongol rulers as uncouth barbarians. Never confident in their role as illiterate conquerors of an ancient civilization, the Mongols devised strict regulations to prevent uprisings. They even banned individual ownership of kitchen knives. Yet the urge for freedom was strong, and plans for revolution were rife. Leaders made secret plans for widespread rebellion, then spread the details to all participants in a most ingenious way. The message "Death to all Mongols on August 15" was written* on tiny slips of paper that were baked in small round cakes. Thousands of people broke open the cakes, read the message, and rose up against their hated rulers. The Yuan dynasty was brought down almost overnight. August 15 is known as the Moon Festival, and to this day is celebrated by eating small round brown cakes that resemble the moon and are called *moon cakes*.

Of all the colors woven into the fabric of Chinese family life, the most important by far is red, *hóng*. The Chinese treasure red far more than do Westerners, to whom red is an aggressive color that means *stop*, warns of danger, or underscores monetary loss. The color red has been symbolic of Communism since the middle of the nineteenth century, when the Communist party was founded. Russian Communists took up the color, and passed it on to the Chinese as a symbol of the revolutionary political philosophy. During the cold war, Americans referred to the Communist regime as Red China.

Red was indeed symbolic of revolutionary values. It represented progress, dynamism, and revolutionary character. In the last chapter we mentioned *Hóng Wèi Bīng*,

紅
hóng
(red)

---

*Anywhere else in the world, it would probably have been whispered from person to person. How the Chinese love the written word!

Red Guards, those fanatical young people who kept revolutionary fervor alive, but left vicious destruction of lives and property in their wake. The official newspaper of the Chinese Communist party is *Hóng Qí*, Red Flag, and the national flag itself is red with five yellow stars.

The Chinese love of red goes back further than any recent political events. For dozens upon dozens of generations, this color has marked joyous celebrations. A Chinese bride wears a red dress on her wedding day. Money given as a gift, especially on New Year's Day, is tucked in little red envelopes. Red candles are burned on festive occasions, like weddings and birthdays.

When an actor, singer, or artist is famous, the Chinese say, *"Tā hěn hóng,"* literally *He is very red.* Of superstars it is said, *"Hóng dé fā zǐ,"* He is so red (famous), *he is beginning to look purple.*

In the East, white represents purity, but it is also the color of mourning. Many Asians wear white at funerals, not black. *Xuě bái,* or *snow white,* is used to describe exquisite purity of teeth, skin, or clothes. Black has unpleasant connotations in China, but not to the same extent as in the West. A mean, greedy person is described as *hēi xīn,* or *black heart,* while a *hēi diàn, black inn,* described in novels, is a fearsome place where innkeepers rob and kill their hapless guests. The Cantonese refer to illegal gangster activity as *hēi shè huì,* or *black society.*

Gray is a dismal color in both East and West. When someone is discouraged or defeated, the Chinese say, *"Tā hě huī xīn,"* He has a gray heart. Yellow is never equated with cowardice in China, but pornographic books are called *huáng sè xiǎo shuō*, *yellow novels*.

Ask any grown child of a Chinese-speaking mother what proverbs she used, and you are sure to get a nostalgic response. Proverbs are a legacy of traditional wisdom Chinese parents give their children to help them cope with the difficulties of life. Some are quotations from ancient works, some refer to folktales or historical events. Usually four-word phrases, proverbs are often framed in the condensed literary style known as *wényán*, discussed in Chapter 4. Ten gems of proverbial lore are presented below.

Proverb

愛	屋	及	烏
ài	*wū*	*jí*	*wū*
(love)	(house)	(extend)	(crow)

Translation: If you love a house, you love its crows (perched on the roof).

This saying is similar to the English phrase "Love me, love my dog."

Proverb

zhòng	*guā*	*dé*	*guā*
(plant)	(melon)	(gain)	(melon)

Translation: If you plant melons, you reap melons.

You get what you deserve, or, to quote the Bible, "... for whatsoever a man soweth, that shall he also reap" (Galatians 6:7).

Proverb

掩	耳	盗	鈴
yǎn	*ěr*	*dào*	*líng*
(cover)	(ear)	(steal)	(bell)

Translation: The thief covers his ears while stealing the bell.

Recalling the notion that a frightened ostrich sticks its head in the sand, this proverb describes a thief who makes off with a bell that rings as he runs. In a vivid image of self-deception, he covers his ears, pretending there is no sound at all.

Proverb

同	床	異	夢
tóng	*chuáng*	*yì*	*mèng*
(same)	(bed)	(different)	(dream)

Translation: The same bed, but different dreams.

Single members of a couple or close associates have very different objectives.

Proverb

塞	翁	失	馬
sài (frontier)	*wēng* (old man)	*shī* (lose)	*mǎ* (horse)

Translation: The old man living at the frontier lost his horse.

An old story, portraying the philosophical attitude of many Chinese, explains this proverb. When an old man lost his horse, his friends came to grieve with him. "Don't pity me," he told them, "for this may not be bad fortune." A few days later, the horse returned to its stable, followed by several wild horses. This time, neighbors came to congratulate him, but he told them, "Don't be overjoyed; this good fortune may bring calamity." Soon afterwards, his only son fell off one of the wild horses, broke his leg, and became a cripple. The old man accepted the disaster calmly, knowing it could be a blessing in disguise. After several years, a war broke out. All able young men were drafted and sent to their deaths on the battlefield. The old man's son, because of his lame leg, remained at home to care for his father until death took the old man.

Although the old man's philosophical attitude is their ideal, the Chinese, like people everywhere, usually comfort themselves with a stoical proverb when disaster strikes and rejoice unequivocally in good fortune.

Proverb

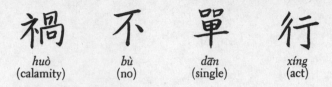

禍	不	單	行
huò	*bù*	*dān*	*xíng*
(calamity)	(no)	(single)	(act)

Translation: Calamities do not occur singly.

As the English saying goes, "It never rains but it pours."

Proverb

虎	父	無	犬	子
hǔ	*fù*	*wú*	*quǎn*	*zǐ*
(tiger)	(father)	(no)	(dog)	(son)

Translation: Tigers do not breed dogs.

Again, there is a rough English equivalent, "Like father, like son."

Proverb

掛	羊	頭	賣	狗	肉
guà	*yáng*	*tóu*	*mài*	*gǒu*	*ròu*
(hang up)	(sheep)	(head)	(sell)	(dog)	(meat)

Translation: He advertises mutton, but sells dog's flesh.

In spite of his respectable façade, that man is engaged in illegal or disreputable activity.

Proverb

寧	為	雞	口	不	為	牛	後
nìng (would rather)	*wéi* (act)	*jī* (chicken)	*kǒu* (mouth)	*bù* (not)	*wéi* (act)	*niú* (ox)	*hòu* (behind)

Translation: Better be a cock's beak than a bull's rump.

Milton said it another way: "To reign is worth ambition though in hell: Better to reign in hell than serve in heaven" (*Paradise Lost,* Book I, 262–63).

Proverb

近	朱	者	赤	近	墨	者	黑
jìn (close)	*zhū* (ver- million)	*zhé* (person)	*chì* (red)	*jìn* (close)	*mò* (Chinese ink stick)	*zhé* (person)	*hēi* (black)

Translation: If you touch vermilion, you get stained red; if you touch ink, you get stained black.

One takes the color of one's company.

Proverbs are but one facet of Chinese traditional wisdom. The next chapter will examine some words from

China's venerable store of scientific knowledge: words of astronomy, calendar making, medicine, and numbering. Chapter 6 also considers the profound impact modern Western science and technology have made upon the Chinese language, and shows how the language for many years handicapped the development of efficient mass communication.

Six

OLD WISDOM, NEW TECHNOLOGY, AND THE CHINESE LANGUAGE

The earliest Chinese scientists, like the astronomers of Egypt and the builders of Stonehenge, turned their attention skyward, trying to understand and predict events vital to their daily lives: the sun's travel, the moon's phases, the seasons' march. A developing society needs time measurements to mark religious observances, to regulate working life, and to record historical events. So primitive astronomers around the world observed the celestial clock and soon came to understand some universal phenomena, which they described and explained in the particular words of their culture.

They learned, for example, that a lunar year, based on a count of the periods between new moons, does not agree with a solar year, measured by the rising and setting sun and by cyclical variations in day length. A calendar derived from the lunar cycle will not forecast seasonal changes, and a calendar based on the sun's seeming rotation around the earth will not predict the phases of the moon, that first observed, elemental rhythm so important to people who don't have street lights. Astronomers of the Shang dynasty (ca. 1766–ca. 1122 B.C.) probably adopted a complicated system to compensate for this discrepancy, the same system later discovered independently by a Greek astronomer named Meton. From oracle bone inscriptions, we know for certain that they set the length of a solar year at 365¼ days and a lunar month at 29½ days. Every once in a while, they would stick an extra month into the year to keep the lunar and solar cycles in phase.

Somehow, during the chaotic twilight of the Zhou dynasty around the third century before Christ, astronomers using only an upright pillar standing against the sky conceived a more accurate calendar they called *yīn-yáng lì* or *lunar-solar calendar*. To begin with, these early calendar makers imagined that the sun circled the earth—a belief shared by most Western astronomers before Copernicus. Visualize a large, flat ring girding the earth's equator, with the sun moving around its outer rim. Chinese astronomers divided this ring into twenty-four equal segments of fifteen degrees each, totaling the 360 degrees of a complete circle. The calendar system they devised depended on two of these "half-month" segments equaling one lunar month.

All twenty-four made up a solar year.

The poetic names assigned to these half-months, listed in Table 6.1, reflect ancient climatic conditions of the Yellow River and areas to its north. Note that half-months beginning the spring and fall equinox and the summer and winter solstice were named for these important seasonal changes. Because the Twenty-four Periods are based on the sun's movement, they can be accurately dated according to the Western calendar.

Yet there is still the *yīn*, or *lunar*, part of the calendar to consider. Even after the establishment of the Twenty-four Periods, the Chinese retained the lunar calendar which measured a year as twelve lunar months of twenty-nine or thirty days each. The first of these months, beginning at *spring starts*, was called, with consummate unpoetic practicality, *Yīyuè*, *First Month*, the next, *Èryuè*, *Second Month;* the next, *Sānyuè*, *Third Month;* and so on. The old discrepancy remains, however. One-twelfth of a solar year is about 30.4 days, while the period between new moons is 29¼ days. Eventually, the two systems get out of phase, and unless some measures are taken, the first day of the first month, New Year's Day, would occur during *great heat* instead of *spring starts*, where it belongs. To prevent this confusion, Chinese astronomers repeat a month every three years, so that one year might have two Augusts, while three years later there might be two Septembers.

With this calendar, festivals like the early April equivalent of All Soul's Day, *Gīngmíng*, and Ten-ten Day, the tenth day of the tenth month, and, of course, New Year's

Table 6.1. The Twenty-four Climatic Periods

Beginning	Chinese	Pīnyīn	Meaning
Feb. 5	立春	lìchūn	spring starts
Feb. 20	雨水	yǔshuǐ	rain water
March 7	驚蟄	jīngzhé	scared insects
March 22	春分	chūnfēn	vernal equinox
April 6	清明	qīngmíng	clear and bright
April 21	谷雨	gǔyǔ	grain rains
May 7	立夏	lìxià	summer starts
May 22	小滿	xiǎomǎn	grain fills
June 7	芒種	mángzhǒng	grain in ear
June 22	夏至	xiàzhì	summer solstice
July 8	小暑	xiǎoshǔ	small heat
July 23	大暑	dàshǔ	great heat
Aug. 9	立秋	lìqiū	autumn starts
Aug. 24	處暑	chǔshǔ	limit of heat
Sept. 9	白露	báilù	white dew
Sept. 24	秋分	qiūfēn	autumn equinox
Oct. 9	寒露	hánlù	cold dew
Oct. 24	霜降	shuāngjiàng	frost falls
Nov. 8	立冬	lìdōng	winter starts
Nov. 23	小雪	xiǎoxuě	little snow
Dec. 7	大雪	dàxuě	heavy snow
Dec. 22	冬至	dōngzhì	winter solstice
Jan. 6	小寒	xiǎohán	small cold
Jan. 21	大寒	dàhán	great cold

Day, could be expected to fall during the same season every year. Prediction allowed for orderly planning.

The *yīn-yáng lì* was used continuously in China until the overthrow of the Qing dynasty in 1912. The new republic, eager to keep up with the West, adopted the Gregorian calendar, introduced to Europe by Pope Gregory XIII in 1582 and now spread throughout the world. The Chinese named its twelve months after their own lunar months. January became *Yīyuè*; February, *Éryuè*; March, *Sānyuè*; and so on.

While the Gregorian calendar is good for planning summit conferences, arranging airline flights, and making production schedules, the *Yīn-yáng lì* still serves to mark the traditional rhythms of Chinese life, so that many Chinese live by two calendars. A top-notch San Francisco secretary for a Caucasian-owned firm, born in Shanghai just before the war, will use the Western calendar to schedule her boss's business meetings, yet celebrate her own birthday according to the old Chinese calendar.

Chinese fortune-tellers reckon astrological calculations by the ancient calendar, and all the traditional festivals are celebrated on their Chinese month and day. Because the months of the *yīn-yáng lì* are based on lunar cycles, its dates vary relative to the Gregorian calendar from year to year. The New Year, for example, or the August 15 Festival (the fifteenth day of the eighth month), commemorating the overthrow of the Mongols, will not always fall on the same "Gregorian" day every year. Whenever there is danger of confusion, the Chinese clarify a given date by saying, for example, "That's April 8 according to the Chinese calendar," or "That's April 8 according to the Western calendar."

In addition to the system of half-months, early Chinese astronomers devised a zodiac based not on the sun's supposed yearly movement through the constellations, as the Western zodiac is, but on a repeating twelve-year cycle. Each year in the cycle is named for an animal which serves as a sign to augur personality traits, as well as to determine the fate of everyone born in that year. The twelve animal signs are: Rat, Ox, Tiger, Rabbit, Dragon, Snake, Horse, Sheep, Monkey, Cock, Dog, and Pig. When the Year of the Pig ends, the cycle begins all over again with another Year of the Rat.

When executing an astrological chart, Chinese fortune-tellers begin with the birth year, but, like Western astrologers, they need to know the date, hour, and minute of birth to make a complete prediction. The animal signs serve not only fortune-tellers and their clients, but ordinary people, who use them to remember the age of children, nieces and nephews, and grandchildren. A Western member of a large family may have trouble keeping track of birth years, but a Chinese in a similar situation finds it easier. All he has to do is associate each relative with an animal sign. Since each sign repeats once every twelve years, there is not much chance of making an error.

Would you like to know your animal sign? The chart in Appendix 3 will tell you what it is.

Christian missionaries brought the seven-day week to China, where it soon gained common acceptance, even by the vast majority of Chinese, who, although they were not Christians, called Sunday *Lǐbàitiān,* or *Worship Day.* Monday was then *Lǐbàiyī,* or *First Day* (of the week); Tuesday *Lǐbàièr, Second Day;* and so on. An alternate system was proposed early in this century as a reaction against the Christian way of naming, with the word for *week* being *Xīngqī,* or *Star Period.* Monday then is *Xīngqīyī,* First Day (of the week); Wednesday *Xīngqīsān,* Third Day; Saturday *Xīngqīliù, Sixth Day;* and Sunday *Xīngqīrì,* literally *Week-Sun,* or *Sun Day.* The Communists abolished Christian terminology in 1949, giving the latter system unchallenged supremacy on the Mainland.

Before leaving the vast regions of earth and sky, we should say that the Chinese are credited with inventing the compass, which they call *zhǐ nán zhēn,* or *south-pointing needle.* The legendary Yellow Emperor, Huang-di, was supposed to have made the first compass, but actual written records of its use did not appear until well after his time. We can safely say that the Chinese have used a compass for about three thousand years. Never being great seafarers, the Chinese used the compass mainly as a tool for determining the most favorable site for a building or road. South was considered the best direction; most Chinese homes face that way.

Another early scientific development in China was the counting system still in use today. Traditional Chinese numbers are often printed side by side with Arabic numerals on calling cards, advertisements, and the like. As we saw in Chapter 2, the first three numbers are simple, straightforward ideographs; yet this pattern continued to ten would disintegrate into a confusion of stripes, so cha-

一
yī
(1)

二
èr
(2)

三
sàn
(3)

四
sì
(4)

五
wǔ
(5)

六
liù
(6)

七
qī
(7)

八
bá
(8)

九
jiǔ
(9)

十
shí
(10)

racters express the remaining numbers. The numbers from one to ten, as well as zero, are written in the margin. Note that some numbers may be written in a more complicated manner; for example, another character for *one* is 壹, for *two* is 弍, and for *three* is 叁. These characters are used on checks and similar documents to make forgery difficult.

The characters shown in the margin are then put together to form numbers from ten to ninety-nine, as in the following examples:

shíwǔ	15	(ten plus five)
èrshí	20	(two tens)
shíèr	12	(ten plus two)
qīshíjiǔ	79	(seven tens plus nine)

Beyond ninety-nine, additional symbols are introduced:

零
líng
(0)

yī bǎi	一 百	100
yī qiān	一 千	1,000
yī wàn	一 萬	10,000
shí wàn	十 萬	100,000
yī bǎi wàn	一 百萬	1,000,000

Note that Chinese has a special character for *ten thousand*, but not for *million*, which is written *hundred ten thousand*. Combinations of larger numbers are illustrated below:

一百　　　　100
二百八十四　284
三百零六　　306

Can you write the number 1949? Try copying the characters on a sheet of paper. The correct answer is at the bottom of the page.*

The origins of Chinese medical practice are lost in the farthest reaches of antiquity. The oldest medical work in Chinese classical literature is well over two thousand years old. Though the beginning of Chinese medicine is obscure, the language is not—not to its users, at least. Western medical terms, grafted onto the roots of dead classical language, are often quite literally Greek to the patient. Not so in China, where the words of medicine are taken from everyday language.

If a fellow worker tells you he has *trachoma*, you might mumble, "Oh, that's too bad, but why are you rubbing your eyes?" In Chinese, the same illness is called *shā yǎn*, or *sandy eyes*, a phrase clearly describing its chief symptom, granular formations under the eyelids.

When the Chinese speak of someone unwell, they say, *"Tāde jīngshén bù hěn hǎo,"* His spirit is not very good. When the discomfort of illness makes a person grouchy, the Chinese attribute his bad temper to *gān huǒ*, or *liver fire*. If outside circumstances annoy him further, his *gān huǒ shàng shēng*, or his *liver fire increases*. Characters

---

*There are two ways of expressing this number. It can be either 一千九百四十九 or simply 一九四九

痛
tòng
(ache)

病
bìng
(disease)

for basic symptoms, like *tòng, ache,* may be combined with parts of the body to form exact equivalents of English words for symptoms, like *wèi tòng, stomachache,* or *tóu tòng, headache.*

The character for disease is written in the margin. Note that the same radical, 疒 , is used in both the words *disease* and *ache.*

The word for inflammation is 炎 *(yán), fire* written twice, or as the English phrase goes, *burning with fever.* This character is used to build the words *fèi yán, lung inflammation (pneumonia),* and *nǎo mó yán, brain membrane inflammation (meningitis).*

Other expressive disease names are: *wèi suān,* or *stomach acid (ulcer), má fēng,* or *hemp insanity* (referring to the patient's rough skin), meaning *leprosy,* and *táng niào bìng, sugar urine disease,* for *diabetes.*

Men have long observed that certain diseases affect specific organs. In China, the heart, *xīn,* was considered the site of the mind. When the vessels passing through it were not obstructed, the mind was clear and the body's health would be good. A heartbeat is *xīn tiào,* literally *heart jump.* Someone very sad is described as *shāng xīn (injured heart)* or *xīn suì (heart broken),* just as in English. The Chinese also use *duàn cháng, intestines broken,* as a metaphor for sadness, but here the word for *broken, duàn,* means *sliced into pieces.*

The gall bladder, *dǎn,* is associated with bravery and judgment. If a man is very courageous, he is said to have eaten the gall bladder of a bear or tiger; but a timid man has the gall bladder of a mouse. The word 氣 *(qì),* meaning *air* or *gas* as well as breath from the lungs, has philosophical and aesthetic significance, as we shall see in Chapter 7. When angry feelings overwhelm the body, the Chinese say, *"Wǒ shēng qì,"* I give birth to gas, a gas which expands as passion grows in intensity until *qì sǐ wǒ le, it kills me*. Another kind of pressure is exerted on the brain when a blood vessel ruptures, filling the brain with blood, *xuè*. In English, this condition is called an apoplectic stroke, in Chinese, *nǎo chóng xuè, brain filled with blood*.

Sometimes, as in the West, diseases are named after their place of discovery. An itchy foot fungus, similar to athlete's foot, is known as *Xiānggǎng jiǎo*, or *Hong Kong foot*. Travelers to Hong Kong may well be afflicted with another ailment, *shuí tǔ bù fú, water and earth do not mix*, the Chinese way of describing the body's rebellion against strange foods, new water, an unfamiliar schedule.

The word *doctor* is translated *yīshēng*, literally *one who brings life back*. He may relieve suffering with an operation, *kāi dāo (open with knife)*, using *má zuì*, or *anesthetic*, which literally means to be *numb* and *drunk*.

Traditional Chinese medicine relies on herbal brews, made from ingredients such as foxglove, betel nut, chrysanthemum, lotus, mustard seed, pepper, mango stones, dried scorpions, silkworms, toads or sea slugs, snakeskins, arrowroot, and honey. Some had real potency against disease, some were as ineffective as the phony dragon bones described in Chapter 4. Another traditional method of curing diseases is the two-thousand-year-old art of acupuncture, or *zhēn jiŭ,* which works through fine needles inserted into specific parts of the body. Acupuncture is used as a form of pain suppressant during operations, as well as a cure for chronically painful conditions like rheumatism. It seems to work in some cases, but no one knows exactly how.

There is a sharp contrast between the precision of Chinese medical language and the awkwardness of Chinese adapted to Western science and technology. In modern times, the major advances in science, with resulting technological leaps, have been made in the West. Chinese, as we have seen, is resistant to outside influences, so the task of translating foreign scientific words is difficult at best and impossible at worst.

The word *laser,* an acronym for *light amplification by stimulated emission of radiation,* is a case in point. No such abbreviations are possible without an alphabet, so the Chinese must find other ways to express the laser concept. One way would be to transliterate, or find two words that sound like *laser* when pronounced together. Another approach would string together words describing the phenomenon. There is no standard way of dealing with the problem, and confusion is inevitable. (For the word *laser,* the Chinese have taken the second approach, using a five-character tongue twister that means, roughly, *to be hit, then shoot out light.*)

Just as Western laymen must keep learning new words and phrases to understand discoveries in science and technology, Chinese must keep adopting these new terms into a language highly unsuited to the purpose. For subjects like chemistry and mathematics, where symbols play an important role, there is virtually no substitute but to adopt English letters representing an equation or compound. Many Western scientists look at Chinese or Japanese technical journals and textbooks with amusement, for after an entire paragraph of characters, a term or equation suddenly appears in English (Figure 6.1). The article then continues in characters.

Although this patchwork of English and Chinese is inconvenient and inelegant, its difficulties are not insurmountable. Japan, a technologically advanced nation, has coped with the situation quite well. The Japanese use about 1,900 Chinese characters plus two sets of forty-five phonetic syllable characters, one set for Japanese words, the other for words of foreign origin. The fact that the Japanese written language can deal with words spelled phonetically does make adoption of Western technology easier in Japan than in China.

Outside of a small group of scholars and diplomats, Americans and Europeans in past generations had virtually no desire to find out what was written in Chinese literature or printed in Chinese newspapers. This situation has changed in recent years. As China emerges from years of isolation to take her rightful place in world affairs, interest in Chinese has greatly increased. A tour of the Mainland would be a straightforward way to gain first-hand knowledge about the Middle Kingdom. Besides tourists, there are now many cultural and scientific exchange programs with the West. Because so few Westerners can read Chinese, machine translation from Chi-

在反应达到平衡时，尽管反应物和生成物的浓度保持不变，实际上正反应和逆反应仍在不断地进行，反应并未停止。不过，在单位时间内，每种物质消耗的数量和生成的数量相等，所以化学平衡是一种动态平衡。

我们研究化学平衡是为了掌握化学反应的客观规律性，以便应用化学平衡的原理来衡量某一可逆反应在一定条件下所能进行的最大限度，就是说，了解反应物在一定条件下转变成生成物的最大程度，这对于确定原料的利用率和产品的产率是有现实意义的。究竟有多少反应物转变为产物，可以根据化学平衡常数推算出来。

（二）化学平衡常数

例如，一氧化碳和水蒸气化合成二氧化碳和氢的反应：

$$CO+H_2O \underset{v_2}{\overset{v_1}{\rightleftharpoons}} CO_2+H_2$$

这是一个可逆反应。若以 v_1 和 v_2 分别表示正反应速度和逆反应速度，按质量作用定律，正反应速度与反应物 CO 和 H_2O 浓度的乘积成正比，即

$$v_1=k_1[CO][H_2O]$$

逆反应速度与生成物 CO_2 和 H_2 浓度的乘积成正比，即

$$v_2=k_2[CO_2][H_2]$$

达到平衡时，正反应速度和逆反应速度相等，即

$$v_1=v_2$$

则
$$k_1[CO][H_2O]=k_2[CO_2][H_2]$$

$$\frac{[CO_2][H_2]}{[CO][H_2O]}=\frac{k_1}{k_2}$$

k_1 和 k_2 分别是正反应和逆反应的速度常数，在一定温度下，它们都是常数，那么两个常数的比值也是常数，可用 K 表示，则得

· 37 ·

Fig. 6.1. A page from a chemistry textbook published in the People's Republic of China.

nese to English offers the only realistic hope of giving the West ready access to what is going on in China. (Of course, one has to analyze and interpret what one reads from a Chinese newspaper, but this can be done in English.)

Computers have been recognized as a tool for translating one language into another for many years. In the present state of the art, many European languages, including Russian, can be routinely translated into English. From the onset, machine translation of Chinese into English met with problems not found in other cases. Because the Chinese language lacks an alphabet, the machine must be provided with a description, in code, of every character in the sentence to be translated. No one has yet built a machine that can read Chinese characters, so the coding must be done manually. Besides being slow and tedious, the process also requires the operator to be familiar with Chinese. Many Chinese words are composed of two characters, as shown in Chapter 2, and combinations of three and four characters are common in literary and technical Chinese. The meaning of a combination of characters is often not obvious from its elements. In spite of the intense research now focused on machine translation of Chinese into English, no satisfactory system has yet been developed.

Western technology is founded on swift access to information, which once depended solely on the alphabet. Before the Internet, an enemy who could obliterate our sense of alphabetical order, destroying easy access to telephone books and indices, could probably overrun us.

Lacking an alphabet, Chinese also lacks alphabetical order, and is at a distinct disadvantage whenever speedy location of printed information is required.

How does a worker in Shanghai look up a friend's telephone number?

The answer: It isn't easy.

Fortunately, there are only about four hundred surnames, and only one hundred of them see widespread use. Surnames are arranged according to the number of strokes needed to write each one. In a city as large as Shanghai (about 12 million people), our worker may have to flip through twenty or thirty pages of the same surname to find his friend. He must first count the number of strokes in his friend's surname, find it, then repeat the process with the middle given name and then the last name.

A Chinese dictionary is more complicated, for it includes all the words of the language, not just four hundred surnames. There are over five hundred words alone written with seven strokes. The Chinese rely on radicals, discussed in Chapter 2, as the primary organizing tool for dictionaries, indexes, and card catalogues. There is no standard order for listing radicals; the information-seeker must learn the system of the particular book or index he is using.

For example, a Chinese unfamiliar with the meaning of the character 海 would look first in a dictionary for a section grouping all the words containing the *water* radical 氵. Words incorporating the same radical are further arranged by the number of strokes in the non-radical part. In the word 海 , the non-radical part, 每 , has seven strokes, and would be listed with other seven-stroke characters using 氵 as a radical.

Obviously, this method is slower than one relying on alphabetical order. Research in library card catalogues is equally encumbered. The old "dictionary catalogue," or alphabetically arranged card file of authors, titles, and subjects for books available in a particular library, is a recent Western development. The Chinese could not use it, for they had no alphabet, but that did not prevent them from arranging libraries. In fact, until the modern era, the Chinese had a greater need for book classification schemes than did Western bibliophiles, for they had a greater number of books.

During the culturally fertile Han dynasty (202 B.C.– 220 A.D.), a complicated scheme of seven divisions was originated and then refined into a classification of books in four divisions: classics, philosophy, history, and literature. Used by the Chinese since the third century A.D., this system preceded the modern Dewey Decimal and Library of Congress systems of subject classification by seventeen centuries.

Arranging books and manuscripts according to subject is the most basic method for organizing libraries, but when collections enlarged enormously after the development of printing, an alphabetical index was needed if one item was to be easily found; the Chinese were prevented by their language from taking this last step toward increased efficiency. The situation has considerably improved, however, with the introduction of Pīnyīn Romanization.

The Western alphabet's supremacy as a tool for locating information extends to communication. For years, the printing press, the telegraph, the typewriter, and now the word processor and e-mail have made written communication so easy that people sometimes pay little attention to *what* they are communicating.

Johann Gutenberg's edition of the Bible printed on paper with movable type is recognized as an important milestone in the path of world history. Books, newspapers, and pamphlets rolled from presses that grew in number and complexity with succeeding generations, printed matter that would educate the common people and change the course of history. The invention of printing, truly a global achievement, was accomplished with some help from the Middle Kingdom.

To begin with, China gave the world paper, a cheap surface for printing (more on this in the next chapter). Then, China produced the world's oldest known printed book, unearthed in 1900 under circumstances as dramatic as the discovery of the Shang oracle bones.

The city of Dunhuang in Gansu Province lies beyond the Gobi Desert, south of the Mongolian border, in one of the least traveled regions of the modern world. Once, when camels carried silk from old Cathay to ancient Rome, it was a thriving settlement along the caravan trail that came to be known as the "Silk Route."

In 1900, at the Caves of the Thousand Buddhas, a fifteen-hundred-year-old religious shrine cut from the cliffs near Dunhuang, a Daoist priest engaged in a restoration project discovered a brick wall that concealed a secret chamber stuffed with paper manuscripts. Later archaeologists realized the importance of this cache, preserved in the bone-dry climate of northwestern China. Not one dated piece of writing in that cave was later than 996 A.D.

A British archaeologist, Aurel Stein, examined some of the manuscripts in 1907, and found one scroll not handwritten but printed. It was a Buddhist scripture called the Diamond Sutra, and had been printed from blocks of wood, according to its text, on May 11, 868 A.D., as a memorial to the parents of one Wang Chieh.

As Thomas Carter says in his seminal work on Chinese printing, the invention of wood-block printing *was* the invention of printing for China and the Far East. Adapting techniques of seal imprinting and stone rubbing,* Chinese craftsmen of the Tang dynasty (618–906 A.D.) developed an improved method for reproducing words and images. They first cut a block of wood to the dimensions of two printed pages, then planed and sized it. A master calligrapher copied the text to be printed on a thin sheet of paper, which was slapped face down on the wooden block. The ink used to write the characters clung to the block, producing a mirror image of the text. A workman with a sharp tool cut away all the wood unmarked by ink, so that the reversed characters stood out in high relief. Then the printing process could begin.

Chinese printers did not use a press; they simply brushed ink on the engraved wooden blocks, pressed thin

---

*These will be described in the next chapter.

paper on the inked surface, brushed it gently with a clean, dry brush, then pulled off a sheet printed on one side. Instead of printing both sides of a sheet, they folded each sheet in half so the blank sides pressed together, then sewed these double pages together with the folded edge out to form a book. Books bound in this way are still available in Chinese bookstores.

Printing was considered nothing more than a handy gimmick for repeating prayers and charms until the years of civil strife following the fall of the Tang dynasty. During this period, known as the Five Dynasties (907–960 A.D.), Sichuan became an independent state with a prime minister named Wu Chao-i. As a student, Wu found his friends unwilling to lend him precious hand-written books, so he vowed that if he ever came into power, he would see that inexpensive books were available to poor scholars. He kept his promise to himself, and ordered classical literature to be printed from wooden blocks.

Meanwhile, another prime minister, Feng Tao, who was skilled and resourceful enough to remain in office during several changes in leadership, wished to project the image of his mini-empire as the one destined to rule China. How best to do this in a country that revered literature? Present the correct text of the Confucian classics, of course. The titles of some of these venerable works, written during the Zhou dynasty (ca. 1122–249 B.C.) and attributed mostly to Confucius, were listed in Chapter 4. Past emperors had ordered them carved in their entirety on tablets of stone.

Lacking both the time and money necessary for that gigantic task, Feng Tao settled for the easier job of printing the classics, and gathered scholars to revise and edit them. The resulting one hundred and thirty printed volumes represent the beginnings of mass communication in imperial China. From then on, printed books took an important place in the Chinese cultural scene as printers refined and improved their art, until, in the Song dynasty (960–1279 A.D.), they produced books of a quality later generations could never equal. Figure 6.2, a page from a book produced toward the end of the Sung dynasty, is an example of their unsurpassed excellence.

During the Song dynasty, Chinese printers experimented with movable type, made first of clay and later of metal. Korean craftsmen picked up on this development, and soon a government printing office and type foundry were established. The Japanese imperial government, too, sponsored printing with movable type. Printing with movable type was abandoned in all three countries—China, Korea, and Japan—when government funding was withdrawn.

How could this happen? Why did China stumble upon one of Western technology's most glittering achievements, only to leave it lying in the dust?

No one knows for sure, but the most obvious answer is: Because of their language. When printing with movable type developed in the West, type founders made twenty-six upper case and twenty-six lower case letters, plus an assortment of punctuation marks, for compositors to set in frames.

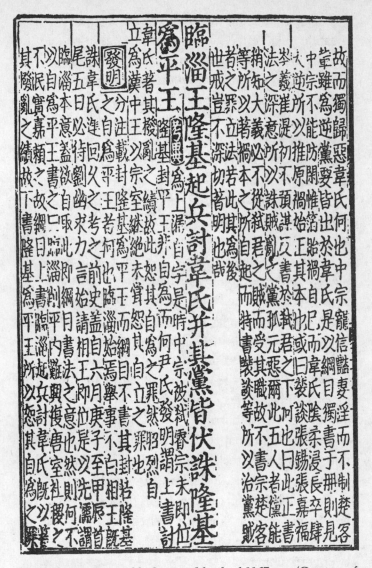

Fig. 6.2. Page from a block-printed book of 1167 A.D. (Courtesy of Newberry Library, Chicago)

Chinese type founders, having no alphabet, were obliged to cast a piece of type for each of the 25,000 or so characters in their language, the investment in metal alone enough to beggar the wealthiest of private publishers. In fact, an eighteenth-century administration facing a shortage of small change, melted down the copper type font for the last major work that was to be printed with movable type in China, a 6,000-volume encyclopedia finished in 1726, and turned it into copper coins. Typesetters couldn't even organize type in manageable-sized cases; arranging and storing so many pieces of type was a task that daunted the most ingenious inventor.*

Types found by the French archaeologist Paul Pelliot in the same cave that yielded the world's oldest printed book prove that simple conservatism played a part in the ultimate rejection of movable type. The wooden types were made in China for printing Uigur script, used by a non-Han people of Central Asia. Uigur script is alphabetic, yet each separate type was cast, following the Chinese practice, not to print *one letter* but an *entire word*.

The last consideration is aesthetic. The Chinese love handwritten script, for reasons we shall explore more fully in the next chapter. Block printing more closely reproduces human handwriting than does printing with movable type, and thus appeals more to the Chinese eye.

---

*In 1313 A.D., a Chinese history of movable type described two revolving tables, each divided into sections for storing type, with a compositor seated between them. One table held characters arranged by rhymes, another the most frequently used characters.

So the Chinese one-upped Gutenberg. They invented movable type first, though they didn't use a printing press. Did any of the European developers of movable type know about the Chinese invention? Probably not, although they may have seen Chinese-printed playing cards, paper money, or religious pictures, and may have known about the abundance of books in China. Paper remains China's only firmly authenticated contribution to Western printing.

Printing presses employing movable type were reintroduced into China from the West at the end of the nineteenth century. Protestant missionaries were the first to cast fonts of Chinese characters for printing religious tracts. In the twentieth century, developments like Linotype and the whole body of photographic printing techniques at last made setting a plate of separate characters easier than carving the same characters out of a single block of wood.

It was not so easy to adapt two other Western communication technologies based on alphabetic languages: the telegram and the typewriter. To send telegrams, the Chinese had to use an ingenious four-digit code of Arabic numerals to represent each zi or character. Now electronic mail, described below, and fax machines have rendered the telegram obsolete. The typewriter, that symbol of Western commerce and journalism for most of the twentieth century, presented formidable challenges to anyone who wanted to type Chinese characters. A Chinese typewriter was an ungainly contraption resting on a large, flat tray of type slugs containing about two thousand characters. A print mechanism would select the character needed, lift it up to strike the character through the inked ribbon, and then return the slug to its proper place. The fastest typist in the East could average no more than twenty characters per minute. The typewriter was an expensive monstrosity used mostly in government offices and large companies. As in the West, computer word-processing programs replaced the typewriter in the last decades of the twentieth century, but with far greater impact on two thousand years of cohesive culture created by the handwritten Chinese language.

Computers in China use the same Roman-alphabet keyboard found in the West. Words must be spelled out in some Romanized version of a spoken language. Everyone in China and even some writers on Taiwan now use the *Pīnyīn* Romanization of Mandarin dialect described at the end of Chapter Two. All over China, children learn to speak Mandarin and write it in *Pīnyīn* Romanization. Once the *Pīnyīn* equivalents of Chinese characters are learned, students are ready to start Chinese word-processing programs. (By the way, Chinese computer programs are written in English.) The writer types in the *Pīnyīn* equivalent for the character wanted, without the accent marks used in this book to indicate tone. A bar on the screen offers a selection of characters, one of which will be the word the writer wants. A mouse-click inserts the character into the document. More sophisticated programs will insert the correct character based on context. Most programs use simplified characters, but a simple command can bring up the traditional, more complicated character.

For example, if we type the word *zhong*, the screen will show some twenty characters all sounding like *zhōng*. As mentioned earlier, many Chinese words are compounds made of two characters. Thus, by a mouse-click we are provided with a list of choices associated with *zhōng* (meaning middle): *zhōngguó* (China), *zhōngwén* (Chinese language), *zhōngxué* (middle school), *zhōngdú* (to be poisoned; here the word is used as a verb), *zhōngnián* (middle age), *zhōngwèi* (a military officer just below the rank of major), and so on. Figure 6.3 shows how Chinese characters look on a computer screen.

Compared to a Western word-processing program, the *Pīnyīn* system of typing and selection is time-consuming and awkward, although it is a great improvement over the clumsy typewriter described above. American children growing up with word-processing aids like spell checkers are becoming increasingly dependent on computers for literacy. But the situation is far worse for Chinese youngsters, who are required to recognize characters but not construct them from scratch. Because word processing has become widespread in China only during the past five years or so, its long-term effect on people's ability to write characters is uncertain. But as neuroscientists have known for years, writing and reading are handled separately by the brain. It may not be long before a whole generation will be able to read and communicate using Chinese characters, but will be unable to write the same characters from memory.

Sending email is a similar process. Romanized Man-

Fig. 6.3 Simplified Chinese characters as they appear on a computer screen.

darin words are typed on the keyboard. Characters show up on the screen and are sent electronically to be read on the receiver's computer screen. Email and the fax machine have had an enormous impact on the way Chinese communicate with one another.

The years Chinese children spent writing the characters with a brush or fountain pen are now spent learning *Pīnyīn* and writing on a computer. After their ancestors for centuries transcribed by hand poetry, stories, petitions to their leaders, or even mundane letters, young Chinese are losing their ability to write characters. This skill has long been considered to be a statement of individual creativity, reflecting the writer's background, education, and personality. Calligraphy, the art described in our last chapter, is losing its paramount position in Chinese culture.

Seven

CHINESE
CALLIGRAPHY

Chinese and American graduate students from Columbia University often go to an uptown restaurant for Chinese food. If we followed a mixed group of these students to their table, we could witness a revealing vignette. The waiter arrives, greets the Chinese habitués in *English*, then departs, leaving a pad of paper and a pencil along with a pot of fragrant tea. To the puzzled Caucasian faces, Harry Liu explains: "He speaks Cantonese only, we speak Mandarin only; so we talk in English and write the order in Chinese."

Following a familiar ritual, the Chinese students keep silent for a moment as the group considers a decision.

Who will write the order?

At last, Harry pushes the pad and pencil in front of David Shen.

"Here, Lao Shen," he says, "you do it. You have the best handwriting."

To David Shen's humble protestations the others nod, affirming that his handwriting is, indeed, superior. In the end he accepts the group's judgment (knowing in his heart it is deserved) and writes their choice of dishes in the most beautiful characters he is able to form with the inadequate tool at his disposal.

Why do the Chinese care about the quality of a mundane restaurant order?

Certainly not because they're afraid they'll get the wrong dish! No, there is a point of personal pride involved. Very few Chinese have, or affect, illegible handwriting. On the contrary, they consider fine handwriting an art they call *shūfǎ* (literally *book-method*), best translated by the English word *calligraphy*.

shū
(book)

fǎ
(method)

In China, this art is held in highest esteem, surpassing painting, sculpture, ceramics, and even poetry. The Chinese passion for the written word was born long before Shang kings wrote questions to their ancestors on oracle bones, and has grown stronger with every passing millennium. Words were so precious that Chinese emperors wrote them on jade tablets, while courtiers made notes after each audience on slates of ivory. Until the Western discovery of printing on a press with movable type, no civilization has produced more written material. Tsien Tsuen-hsuin, after an intensive study of Chinese manuscripts and inscriptions, believes that more books were written and reproduced in China by the end of the fifteenth century A.D. than in all other countries of the world combined.

Writing in China has never been simply a useful tool for communication, but an art in its own right, and one that has generated hundreds of thousands of words of description, appreciation, and criticism. Volumes have been written on aesthetic theory, on training the artist, and on particular virtues of a single calligrapher or piece of calligraphy. Calligraphy has its historians as well, writers who categorize calligraphic styles, tracing development and mutual relationships.

Throughout most of Chinese history, a philosopher's essay, however wise, would be scorned if written in indifferent calligraphy. The Chinese scholar is literally a "man of letters"; all his learning is for naught unless his handwriting is good. Painters are good calligraphers first and good painters second. Even the humblest clerk could gain advancement with fine calligraphy, and captains of industry would be chagrined to reveal that they wrote in a poor hand. Monks of old China might renounce the world, but they would take paper and brushes to their mountain hermitage for the single-minded cultivation of poetry and calligraphy. Prayers, even now, are more often written than spoken. Traditional physicians, far from scrawling prescriptions illegibly, wrote them clearly and beautifully, then ground the paper up in medicinal broth. Men of action found time to practice calligraphy, even on the battlefield—unlike their illiterate Western counterparts, the knights of old—and it is said that a general once capitulated when the request for surrender was composed and copied in a style too lovely to ignore.

Works of Chinese calligraphic art are not reserved exclusively for the educated, rich, and powerful. The most impoverished household can be enriched by a masterpiece of calligraphy. Since good calligraphers rarely live by their handwriting, but earn their rice with another skill, they can afford to share their art with anyone who appreciates it. Wang Xizhi, a general of the fourth century A.D. whose calligraphic achievements put him in the same sublime sphere as Michelangelo, Shakespeare, and Mozart, has been portrayed writing on a poor old woman's fan. She may have rewarded him with the gift of a goose, a bird he loved for its beauty as much as its flavor. Geese were said to have inspired Wang's calligraphy by their graceful flight.

The streets of every Chinese village and town are free and open exhibition galleries of calligraphy. All restaurants, offices, and shops display signboards which proclaim their names and tout excellent goods and services. Inside a new restaurant, diners may feast their eyes on beautifully written scrolls conveying congratulations and wishes for success from the restaurant owner's friends. If the restaurant does well, these scrolls may remain on the walls many years.

Devotees of calligraphy may wander the streets for hours, savoring the public profusion of art. It is impossible to imagine a connoisseur of Western calligraphy doing the same, at least in most American cities and towns. Yet every Chinese person—including shopkeepers, restaurateurs, and businessmen who commission craftsmen to paint the signs—knows that signboard writing is not truly calligraphy. The calligrapher's ink-laden brush flows across paper or silk just once, while signboard painters outline characters first, then paint within the lines. True calligraphy is a living hummingbird, afloat on blurred wings, vibrating with life; a signboard is a stuffed hummingbird, forever still in a museum exhibition case.

Western calligraphy and Chinese calligraphy are as different as the cooking styles of a modern American homemaker and a traditional Chinese housewife. Most Western cooks begin with a recipe that states precise ingredient amounts and exact cooking times. Except for gravies, sauces, and omelets, most of the triumphs of Western cuisine do not demand a cook's complete attention; they roast, bake, or simmer while the cook turns his mind from them. A good dish tastes good in exactly the same way every time it is served.

Chinese cooks rarely follow a recipe, although procedures and techniques are firmly fixed in their minds. They adjust ingredient amounts to the supplies available and the number of people to be served, and measure with their hands or the ends of chopsticks. Most Chinese dishes require the cook's undivided attention: timing is split-second, flavor depends on subtle and rapid changes in texture and temperature. To the Chinese, culinary individuality is a valued commodity. The more skillful the cook, the more able he is to express his identity, subtly but surely, in every dish he cooks. The truly refined palate discerns and appreciates special qualities that make one cook's version of a well-known dish never quite the same as another cook's.

To the Chinese, Western calligraphy is like Western cooking: a bit too mechanical and lifeless in its uniformity. Unfortunately, only a few Westerners appreciate calligraphy as an art form. (In the West, there are many more gourmets than calligraphy aficionados; in China the numbers would be roughly equal.) Although Western calligraphy, particularly the superb italic hand, has enjoyed a renaissance since the early 1960s, never has it reigned supreme above all other arts as calligraphy has for centuries in China.

To the general population of Westerners, good handwriting is something one learns as a child: a clear, rounded hand with symmetry and neatness its greatest virtues. Good handwriting is something great-grandmother had, yet her descendants seem never to learn it. Her copperplate hand, prized by the *McGuffey's Reader* generation, is not true Western calligraphy, though—it is just good handwriting.

Juxtaposing a sample of excellent Western calligraphy, Figure 7.1, with a piece of Chinese calligraphy, Figure 7.2, shows that the two arts are indeed worlds apart. To the Chinese eye, Roman letters are hopelessly invariable. As we saw in Chapter 2, they possess only a few strokes, and these, straight or evenly curved, are not particularly interesting. Western calligraphers practice their letters until they have achieved one perfect form, to be repeated over and over, so that the first *e* on a page looks just like every other *e*. The Chinese find this regularity monotonous and too close to printing to be relished as art.

The Chinese hand finds the pen, even the flexible broad-nibbed instruments used to create fine Western calligraphy, incapable of much variation. The pen can go from thick to thin, it is true, but only one thick and one thin. It does not respond to changes in pressure, nor does it allow variations in moisture or intensity of ink. Letters written with a pen are careful and symmetrical and, to a Chinese, without life, without motion.

Even the quality of attention demanded of the calligrapher is different. A Western calligrapher must pay attention to what he is doing, of course, but his work does not demand the absolute concentration and mental tranquility of his Chinese counterpart. One brush hair out of place can undo a Chinese calligrapher. The Westerner can touch up small mistakes, while revision of Chinese calligraphy is unthinkable. One mistake, and the whole piece is discarded.

The unique beauty of Chinese calligraphy stems from *what* is written — characters — and *how* they are written — with a brush. The combination of brushwork with characters that are both abstract and pictorial produces a medium of expression valued for its vigorous and infinitely variable movement. Chinese calligraphy is a totally spontaneous, highly individualistic art. The Chinese feel that a man's handwriting accurately measures the extent of his cultural attainment and aesthetic sensibilities, and even betrays his physical appearance. One of the most sensitive interpreters of Chinese calligraphy in English, Chiang Yee, looked at the handwriting of a long dead

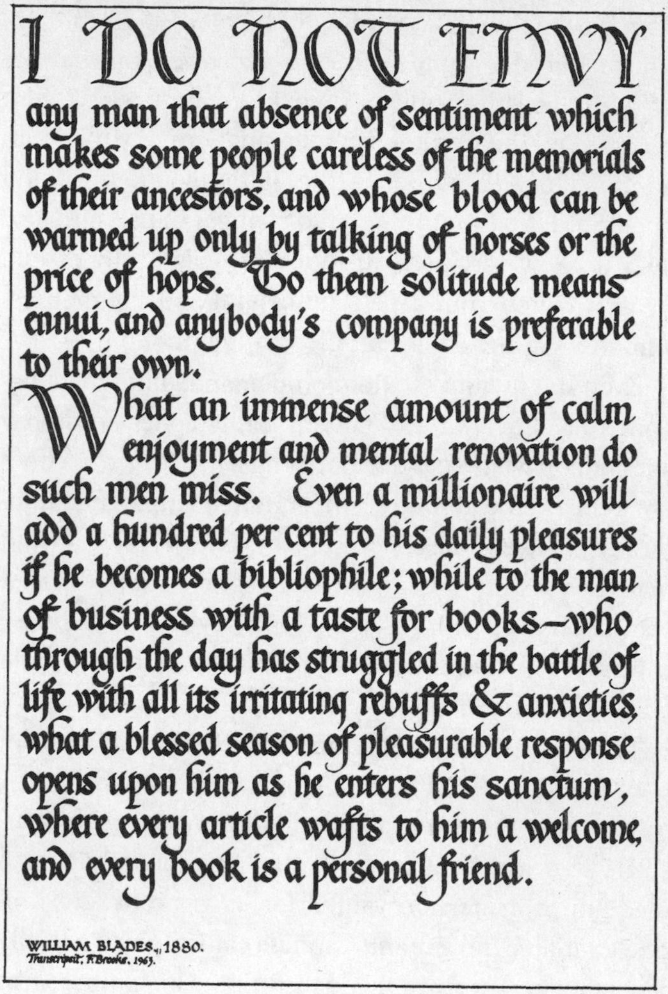

I DO NOT ENVY any man that absence of sentiment which makes some people careless of the memorials of their ancestors, and whose blood can be warmed up only by talking of horses or the price of hops. To them solitude means ennui, and anybody's company is preferable to their own.

What an immense amount of calm enjoyment and mental renovation do such men miss. Even a millionaire will add a hundred per cent to his daily pleasures if he becomes a bibliophile; while to the man of business with a taste for books—who through the day has struggled in the battle of life with all its irritating rebuffs & anxieties, what a blessed season of pleasurable response opens upon him as he enters his sanctum, where every article wafts to him a welcome, and every book is a personal friend.

WILLIAM BLADES, 1880.
Transcript: F.Brooks. 1963.

Fig. 7.1. Sample of excellent Western calligraphy, executed by Florence Brooks. (Courtesy of Chapin Rare Book Library of Williams College)

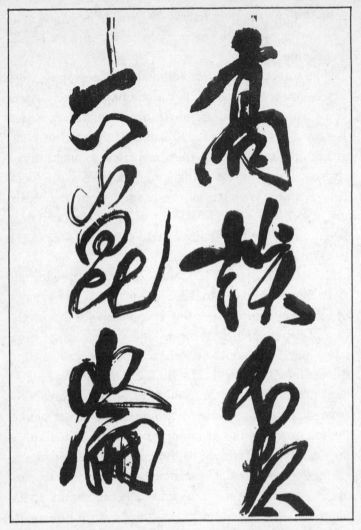

Fig. 7.2. Chinese calligraphy by Fu Shan (1607–1684 A.D.), Qing dynasty. (The Art Museum, Princeton University)

emperor of the Song dynasty (960–1279 A.D.) and said, "His writing shows the emperor to have been a well-built, handsome figure."*

文 房

wén (litera-ture) *fáng* (house)

四 寶

sì (four) *bǎo* (treasure)

The subject of Chinese calligraphy, ideographic characters, has been discussed in earlier chapters; this chapter deals with the technique of Chinese calligraphy, which has two aspects. One is the strokes used to construct characters and the other is the tools used to make these strokes. The Chinese calligrapher has four basic tools, called "Four Treasures of the Study." They are brush, ink, inkstone, and paper. The first three have certainly been used since the Shang dynasty (ca. 1766 — ca. 1122 B.C.), most likely even earlier.

In the Han dynasty (202 B.C.–220 A.D.), the glorious age that gave its name to the Chinese people, the quartet of scholarly treasures became complete with the invention of paper. The most formal styles of calligraphy are taken from inscriptions on stone and bronze made during the earlier Zhou (ca. 1122–249 B.C.) and Qin (221–207 B.C.) dynasties, yet because the brush moves more freely over paper than any other writing surface in use before the Han dynasty, the invention of paper permitted more cursive styles to develop. By the end of the Han dynasty, Chinese characters had reached a form modern readers of Chinese would recognize, and basic calligraphic styles had been established, to be practiced with infinite variations by generations of calligraphers to come.

---

*Chiang Yee, *Chinese Calligraphy: An Introduction to Its Aesthetic and Technique,* 3rd ed. (Cambridge, Mass.: Harvard University Press, 1973), p. 83.

The oldest and most distinctively Chinese of the Four Treasures is the writing brush, or *brush-pen*, as it is sometimes called. The Chinese brush, shown in Figure 7.3, is perfectly round, unlike the flat lettering brushes of Western sign painters. It consists of three basic parts: holder, hair, and sheath. The holder, or handle, is a length of bamboo tube or a hollow wooden rod. The hair, or brush, is constructed in layers. A central bunch of deer or rabbit hair is surrounded by an outer circle of softer hairs taken from goats or wolves. This bundle of hair is tied firmly with silk or hemp string; the tied end is then dipped in lacquer or glue and inserted into the holder. Fine brushes are then covered with a sheath or cap to protect the delicate hairs.

Brushes come in all different sizes. The biggest, large enough to paint a house, is used for billboard-sized characters. The tiniest, the size of a single grain of rice, is used for the most delicate lines. With a brush, the writer can alter the width and strength of strokes because a brush can absorb different quantities of ink and respond to rapid changes in pressure against the paper. With a brush, the writer can create a pleasing symmetry of strokes within each character, and can imbue his writing with the dynamic life of natural forms: rivers, waterfalls, mountains, and leaves. Good brushes may last a lifetime; calligraphers can and do spend fortunes on them, especially when their handles are made of ivory, jade, or gold. An excellent brush is a writer's beloved friend, and calligraphers who outlive their brushes have been known to bury the worn-out tool with great ceremony.

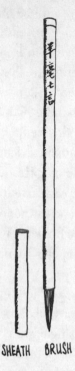

Fig. 7.3. Chinese writing brush.

SHEATH   BRUSH

The Chinese brush is almost certainly as old as the language itself. Pottery five thousand years old, excavated from various sites around northern China, bears decorations of black slip, skillfully applied with a brush. This Neolithic brush is the direct ancestor of all the ones used today. Oracle bone inscriptions were written first with a brush, then incised by a craftsman skillful enough to push his sharp instrument along the wendings of every brush-stroke.

Meng Jian, a Qin dynasty general who supervised

construction of the Great Wall, gets traditional credit for inventing the brush, even though all he really did was make it better. As court historian for Shihuangdi, the Tiger of Qin, his constant use of brushes must have inspired plenty of ideas for improved construction. Brushes in his day were about a foot long and made of bamboo. One of Meng's ideas may have been to substitute a smooth wooden rod for the more awkward bamboo holder.

A brush must be dipped in ink, though Chinese brushes never sink into bottles. Chinese ink is stored and carried as a solid black bar, sometimes incised with decorations and characters traced in gold. This bar, or ink stick, shown in Figure 7.4, is prepared by jelling crushed soot with glue. When ready to write, the calligrapher grinds the bar with a few drops of water on an inkstone until he has achieved his desired consistency.

The stick form allows a writer to vary the ink solution

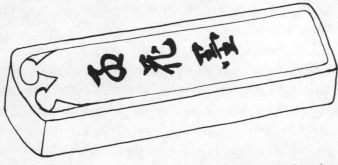

Fig. 7.4. Ink stick.

according to his needs, from blackest black to palest gray. Bottled liquid ink may be more convenient, but it does not allow this flexibility. In the days of the emperors, a scholar kept a young boy called a "scholar-kid" in his household. This little person would fetch and carry, do odd jobs, and grind the scholar's ink. Then as now, an ink stick just six inches long and one inch wide used daily by a calligrapher would last at least a year.

The Chinese have always been master inkmakers. Western artists, who appreciated its quality, have used Chinese ink for centuries, although they call it "India ink." Ink in solid form was probably always used in China. Soot, available wherever fire burns, is obviously good for making black marks. Very early on, controlled burning of tung oil, petroleum, or pine wood was found to produce a fine-grade soot called lampblack, which was then mixed with glue extracted from fish skins or leather by-products. Red ink made from cinnabar was used in the Shang dynasty, particularly for the most important official documents, but its use fell off in later eras, except as an ink for seals.

The invention of ink is traditionally attributed to a calligrapher and inkmaker named Wei Tan, who lived during the late Han dynasty, around the third century A.D. In those days, it was common for the emperor to present favored courtiers with ink. Wei Tan refused the present, preferring to make his own ink, which was said to be most intensely black. Wei Tan's contribution to inkmaking amounted to improvement only, for we know ink was used before the Han dynasty. A recipe handed down since the fifth century A.D., possibly Wei Tan's own, goes as follows:

Fine and pure soot is to be pounded and strained in a jar through a sieve of thin silk. This process is to free the soot of any adhering vegetable substance so that it becomes like fine sand or dust. It is very light in weight, and great care should be taken to prevent it from being scattered around by not exposing it to the air after straining. To make one catty of ink, five ounces of the best glue must be dissolved in the juice of the bark of the *ch'in* tree which is called *fan-chi* wood in the southern part of the Yangtze Valley. The juice of this bark is green in color; it dissolves the glue and improves the color of the ink.

Add five egg whites, one ounce of cinnabar, and the same amount of musk, after they have been separately treated and well strained. All these ingredients are mixed in an iron mortar; a paste, preferably dry rather than damp, is obtained after pounding thirty thousand times, or pounding more for a better quality.

The best time for mixing ink is before the second and after the ninth month in a year. It will decay and produce a bad odor if the weather is too warm, or will be hard to dry and melt if too cold, which causes breakage when exposed to air. The weight of each piece of ink cake should not exceed two to three ounces. The secret of an ink is as described; to keep the pieces small rather than large.*

The inkstone, Figure 7.5, is the companion of the ink stick. Its most basic form, easily found these days at Chinese stationeries and ordinary art supply stores, is a

*Tsien Tsuen-hsuin, *Written on Bamboo and Silk* (Chicago: University of Chicago Press, 1962), pp. 166–67. © 1962 by the University of Chicago. Published in 1962.

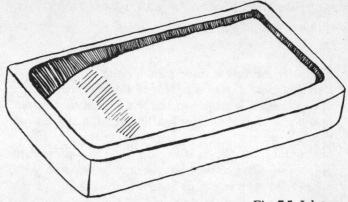

Fig. 7.5. Inkstone.

rectangular black stone with a shallow tray carved in the top. The tray dips down to a trough at one end. The dry ink stick is ground against the flat surface of the tray and mixed with water brushed up from the trough. A good inkstone should be slightly rough and absorbent, but not too rough or too absorbent, for a perfectly smooth inkstone would be unfit for grinding, while an overly porous one would take in all the ink. Because ink was probably solid from the earliest days, it is safe to assume that there was some kind of palette to grind it on, although the oldest known inkstone dates from the Han dynasty. Early calligraphers used inkstones made of earthen bricks, and later generations prized the fine brick tiles from a palace called Bronze Bird, built by Cao Cao in 210 A.D., as well as the smooth stones from Tuan-chi Quarry in Guangdong Province. Inkstones may be had in many shapes and sizes. Some are elaborately carved and decorated, with handsome fittings of wood or lacquer.

Finally, a calligrapher needs paper, the fourth treasure of his retreat. The best paper is handmade, even today, with a coarse texture that will absorb and spread the ink. This rough paper is perfect for a calligraphic style marked by irregularity, asymmetry, and individual eccentricities. The ink-laden brush traveling across its textured surface leaves a line richer for being absorbed and spread; the nearly dry brush skimming its little hills and valleys leaves a strong, roughly broken line. Figure 7.6 is a good example of the perfect union of ink and paper.

Fig. 7.6. Calligraphy by Yao Shou (1422–1495 A.D.), Ming dynasty. (The Art Museum, Princeton University)

Chinese paper is entirely unsuited to pen writing, as many a casual customer of a Chinese stationer discovers when he puts fountain pen to letter paper from Japan or Taiwan. The pen skips and clogs, making a dreadful mess on a surface intended as a vehicle for the brush.

Asians cherish good paper. In Japan, where paper is still made by hand, master papermakers, as holders of "intangible cultural properties," that is, the techniques of papermaking, are designated "Living National Treasures" by a national cultural committee and the Ministry of Education. Japanese paper is tough, slightly stretchy, absorbent, and long-lasting. Natural dyes added during the manufacturing process create a rainbow of muted colors. Because one of its ingredients is mashed fiber from the paper mulberry tree, Japanese paper, or *washi*, is correctly termed "mulberry paper."

The basic steps in making paper are as follows. First, cellulose fibers from trees, grasses, or rags are macerated until every single fiber is separate. These individual fibers are then mixed with water, and lifted from the water in a thin sheet spread over a *mold*, or large, flat screen. Water drains through the screen, and the matted fibers left to dry on the screen's surface become paper. This process, one of China's contributions to world technology, is still the foundation of the most sophisticated machine manufacturing techniques.

The invention of paper in China is accurately recorded as 105 A.D. Before then, characters had been brushed on bamboo, silk, and a kind of quasi-paper produced from silk scraps by a method akin to feltmaking.

Now a woman steps into the scene, one of those women we meet now and then in Chinese history whose brains and strong will repudiate our traditional image of the silent, submissive Asian female. She was the emperor's consort, Madam Deng, crowned empress in 102 A.D. A lover of literature, she scorned the rare and precious gifts she received from other countries on the occasion of her coronation. All she wanted was quasi-paper and ink.

Into this court, where literature and calligraphy were the royal fashion, came Cai Lun, a eunuch placed at the head of an imperial manufacturing office. Unlike Meng Jian and Wei Tan, to whom Chinese tradition gives totally undeserved credit for inventing brush and ink, Cai Lun may actually have invented paper. Although he probably did not spend his nights fiddling around with wet rags, shredded grass, and a mold, he supervised workers who did. He could well have been the person who looked at a pile of silk scraps, discarded fishing nets, hemp, and tree bark, and thought, "There's paper in there."

True paper has been found that may predate Cai Lun, but scholars do not agree on its authenticity, and until more certain evidence is found, the world must, like old-fashioned Chinese papermakers who burned incense before his portrait, honor Cai Lun as the inventor of paper.

The History of the Later Han Dynasty tells us that in 105 A.D. Ts'ai Lun reported the manufacture of paper to the emperor, and that the emperor was pleased enough to ennoble Cai Lun. History does not report Empress Deng's reaction, but she must have prized the new material and may have been one of the first to try her calligraphy on it. Cai Lun's product was called *zhī*, written

紙

zhī
(paper)

絲
sĪ
(silk)

with the radical for *silk*, ever after the word for *paper* in Chinese. (The English word *paper* is rooted in the Latin *papyrus*, a writing material used by the ancient Egyptians which is not true paper.)

Cai Lun did not live to be an old man, basking in the glory of his creation. Years after he first made paper, he was caught in the middle of a court intrigue and had to poison himself, but his invention was a landmark in the history of world communication. Buddhist monks carried the papermaking process to Korea and Japan in the fourth and fifth centuries A.D. Merchants and bureaucrats moved it slowly westward, and Chinese papermakers captured by Moslem troops in a battle fought in Turkestan (extreme western China) in 751 A.D. taught the craft to their captors. The Moslems began manufacturing paper in Samarkand, where bounteous fields of flax and hemp and plenty of pure water encouraged the production of superior paper.

By 1300, when Italy stood on the threshold of the Renaissance, the technique had reached Fabriano, Italy, still an important center of Italian papermaking. In another hundred years, paper was manufactured in Nuremberg, Germany, and half a century later it was found to be the best surface for receiving ink off newly discovered movable type. From then on, history would never be the same. Men's minds would be swayed increasingly by printed words—Luther's Five and Ninety Theses, the King James Bible, the Declaration of Independence, *Das Kapital*—to great deeds and monstrous ones. Yet printed words would have remained exclusively for the wealthy

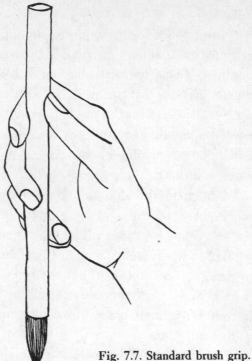

Fig. 7.7. Standard brush grip.

few without a cheap, easily made surface for printing: paper.

We have traveled far from the Chinese scholar's retreat. Now is the time to return there, following in our mind's eye a path of stepping-stones through his garden, around a pond filled with golden carp,* into his study,

*Goldfish, first domesticated in China, are called *jīn yú* in Chinese.

where we will learn some basic techniques of Chinese calligraphy.

A calligrapher begins by picking up his brush. Not all calligraphers hold the brush in exactly the same way, but beginners should start with the standard grasp shown in Figure 7.7. Note that the brush is always held straight up; it never slants against the paper. To write Chinese properly, Westerners must unlearn their habitual "pencil" grip, good for holding chopsticks but not for wielding Chinese brushes.

Wang Xizhi, the aforementioned goose-loving calligrapher, believed that a firm grip on the brush was essential to creating superior calligraphy. He crept behind his young son while the boy practiced calligraphy and tried to snatch away the brush, but the son's grip remained tight. When the father could not pull the brush away, he happily and accurately prophesied that his son would be a great calligrapher.

The wrist rests on the table when small and medium-sized characters are being written. To form larger characters, the wrist and elbow sweep above the table, providing greater freedom of movement. Calligraphy can be a strenuous exercise that many Chinese practice early in the morning, when Westerners might jog or play several sets of tennis. Perhaps the arm and shoulder exercise involved in long sweeps across the paper helps Chinese calligraphers, like Western orchestra conductors, to attain a healthy longevity.

Strokes of the brush are used to build each character, as noted in Chapter 2, where basic strokes were shown.

These strokes are the most fundamental linear element of calligraphy, an art that exalts the beauty of line. The subject of strokes alone has elicited volumes of description and criticism from Chinese writers over the centuries. When judging a piece of calligraphy, the Chinese look for two important qualities. One is the strength, or *gú (bone)*, of each stroke. Strength does not mean that the brush must be pressed hard against the paper all the time. Strength refers to the right emphasis at the right place. Bad calligraphy is called "fleshy," for it has an overly soft quality Americans might term "spineless."

The other essential quality of good calligraphy is *qì*, or *life movement*, the cosmic spirit that animates all natural forms. The comparison of painted signboard and stuffed hummingbird made earlier in this chapter was not an idle choice. Chinese calligraphy, like the rest of Chinese art, has from its beginning drawn inspiration from nature.

Cang Jie, the Middle Kingdom's legendary inventor of writing, observed the patterns written in the heavens by the movements of stars and planets, the footmarks birds print in the dust, and the designs inscribed on tortoise shells, then used nature's lines to express spoken words. Chinese writers on calligraphy since the Han dynasty constantly compare writing with natural activity, as in the following passage written by a calligrapher of the Tang dynasty:

In writing one sees the "hanging needle," the dropping dew; crashing thunder, falling rock, flying bird, startled beast. Heavy as breaking clouds, light as the cicada's wings, graceful as the new moon, independent as the stars—it equals the exquisiteness of nature and is not to be accomplished by human effort.*

The life-force crucial to good calligraphy cannot be achieved through reason or through lengthy, tedious craft. A calligrapher is like a diver poised on the highest springboard. All his training, all his practice, must be totally integrated with the fiber of brain and muscle so that one push-off and a few deft twists will achieve perfection of form.

To the uninitiated observer watching the brush slide over the paper with never a backtrack, this perfection looks deceptively simple. Yet years of training lie behind the apparently effortless motion. When China was an empire, children learned to write with a brush. No other tool was offered. Now they start with a pencil and begin calligraphy lessons later because it is no longer compulsory in school.

Once a student has learned to hold his brush properly, he traces large characters printed from the work of master calligraphers, using the boundaries of the ninefold square, shown on the next page, as guides for each character. The ninefold square is a teaching aid designed to help the novice compose a character. While it is not possible or even desirable to make all characters exactly the same dimension, the guidelines help a young calligrapher limit over-all character size and attain a proper balance within

*Lucy Driscoll and Kenji Toda, *Chinese Calligraphy* (New York: Paragon Book Reprint Corp., 1964), p. 15.

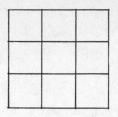

the character. Dividing a square into thirds rather than quarters or halves encourages the asymmetry so valued by Chinese calligraphers.

The framing lines, described in Chapter 2, are used for an entirely different purpose. Framing is a structural device that clearly distinguishes each element of a character, while the grid of the ninefold square is an aid to artistic composition.

At this stage, characters are written in *regular script* (see Figure 7.10), a style marked by distinct, even strokes. A student might trace five to fifty characters a day. After some practice, the student graduates to making strokes freehand, then begins to write characters of his own, without tracing, but usually with a printed character as a model. When proficient at forming characters within the large square, a Chinese schoolchild begins to write smaller characters, each occupying just one of the nine squares. Small characters are written in the same way as large characters but control must be greater because of the reduced area. Without marks inside the small squares to guide his brush, the young calligrapher must marshal his newly learned composition skills.

The proportions of the ninefold square determine the

relative size of large and small characters. Banners, shop signs, and wall posters take large characters, while characters one-ninth that size are used for letters and documents.

If he is destined to be a good calligrapher, a young scholar writes adequate regular script after several years of practice. From his brush flow strokes with authority, strokes that stand each word firmly on its feet. Then he is ready to explore new territories of calligraphic style.

Over the centuries, Chinese experts on calligraphy have classified dozens of different scripts, and no master calligrapher is content to use only one of them for all his work. The study and mastery of various styles is crucial to a calligrapher's training. The many different styles can be grouped into five categories, presented in order of increasing flexibility. The earliest, *seal writing,* encompasses all the styles extant before the Han dynasty: *shell and bone,* taken from the pictorial characters incised on oracle bones; *large seal,* found mainly in inscriptions on bronze and stone during the Zhou dynasty; and *small seal,* the standardized style imposed on China by the Tiger of Qin, Shihuangdi. During the past two thousand years, calligraphers have gone back to these ancient styles, represented here by a sample of large seal script, Figure 7.8, that came from the underbelly of the Shang rhinoceros shown in Figure 4.3.

The old scripts are also used for the seals that adorn Chinese scrolls. We will speak of seals again when the subject of painting comes up. Seal writing is the least flexible of Chinese styles. Because ancient characters were

Fig. 7.8. Large seal script. Rubbing from bronze vessel in the shape of a rhinoceros, Shang dynasty. (Asian Art Museum of San Francisco. The Avery Brundage Collection)

carved into bone, bronze, and stone, they lack the variation in stroke width a brush makes possible.

The next calligraphic style, *official writing*, Figure 7.9, developed after the Tiger of Qin's small seal writing as a kind of shorthand for clerks and government officials. Although it is a stolid, precise style, some variations are

Fig. 7.9. Official script by Jin Nong (1687–1764 A.D.), Qing dynasty. (Collection John M. Crawford, Jr., New York)

余盡此卷自乙丑艤海吳江舟次無事檢得此紙計共六幅
接為長軸始落墨也自吳赴松江將匝月矢未及為
尺有好事者已聞之畫玄宰先生及見先生素觀善志乃迂
而辭舟泊白龍潭先了前一紙抽見先生然頭不語久弃而
問也曰山高韓秀林翠衣人不回兩有趣迤之風此何
圖也可同讀陸機左思拓隱詩有興于懷將構是圖得夜半方起
酌豪欲劇談因論及世未销耳先生闢之解
索之而歸是歲十月後曾玄宰先生于吳江忽訏余曰同來得
此卷之後又聞得義眉丘整耕得義頌烟雲余且了生平
山侶志未竟也令將借硯田以隱為抒懷過志亦呈了生平
蓋世人于出處之際不能割裂以世念未销半方
盡亦有心人也言畢謝退歸事筆墨若忘歲月此卷計成
雖九易釵晦病恙相半及病起泰日未克為塵所妨蓋斯
澗蓋亦朔晦病恙相半每至落日孫硯挑燈絶不飲
酒鼎徵索者命煩亂不敷草每至落日孫硯挑燈絶不飲
應索者松花餅茗葉湯其氣芬研墨神將倦遂闢筆
或東燭看花或捲簾對月其剔撥荼越子丑而方罷為累其
功不二月也曰招隱圖并賦五言二十韻書于卷末我固知世風
絶俗遯趣曰招隱圖并賦五言二十韻書于卷末我固知世風
人皆非隱者也皆思隱而未嘗隱能者也憶嘗我其必有先
我而隱之者矢我招隱可也即曰自招亦我招隱可也即自招
亦無不可也我將隱朝市而不得隱陵載而不得將隱于詩
盡而詩畫已散落人間又不得收拾姓字矢亦懷此而善藏
以俟夫同志者

Fig. 7.10. Regular script by Xiang Shengmo (1597–1658 A.D.), Ming dynasty. (Los Angeles County Museum of Art, Museum purchase)

beginning to occur as brush and writing surfaces improve. Official writing was followed by a third style, evolved during the Han dynasty, known as *regular script,* Figure 7.10, the standard style of calligraphy still in use today. As mentioned earlier, this style is the one children learn first, as well as the basis for type design.

Regular style is the starting point for *running style,* Figure 7.11, conceived late in the Han dynasty. Here the brush is supreme, traveling rapidly over paper or silk, curving around corners, jumping away at the end of a stroke. This faster, freer style serves the Chinese as an everyday handwriting style for manuscripts, letters, and grocery lists.

The fifth style, *cursive,* Figure 7.12, is an even quicker, less deliberate script, favored by impetuous spirits. Cursive style originated during the Han dynasty and became highly popular in later eras. Characters written in cursive style run together so the reader can barely make them out. Legibility is not considered as important to this style as the abstract beauty of pure line, imbued with the passion of life-force.

Probably the earliest sample of manuscript calligraphy available appears as a collection of wood and bamboo strips written in the first and second centuries A.D. by minor bureaucrats on the edge of the Han empire. Buried until the early twentieth century, these messages from the past can still be read by literate Chinese. Only a few samples of brushwork by early masters remain today, for wars, rebellions, and conquests destroy works of art as surely as natural accidents like earthquakes and floods.

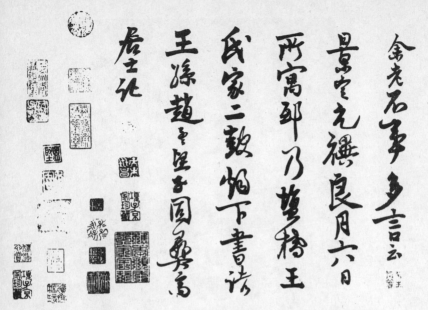

Fig. 7.11. Running script attributed to Zhao Mengjian (1199–1267 A.D.), Song dynasty. (Collection John M. Crawford, Jr., New York)

China certainly had her share of these calamities.

Consider the history of China's stellar piece of calligraphy, written by the goose-loving master Wang Xizhi on the occasion of an outdoor gathering in a spot known for its unusual beauty. The philosophical essay he composed and wrote after drinking several cups of wine was immediately recognized as a masterpiece that even the master himself could not duplicate later, no matter how hard he tried. Many copies were made, and the original was lost for a time, only to be discovered, some say, during the Tang dynasty (618–906 A.D.) in the secret collection of a monk. A Tang emperor coveted the piece, appropriated

Fig. 7.12. Cursive script by Chen Xian-zhang (1428–1500 A.D.), Ming dynasty. (Asian Art Museum of San Francisco. The Avery Brundage Collection)

it for his own collection, and had it burned with him. Whether this story is true or not, the piece has not been seen since the Tang dynasty.

Because paper is so easily moved and destroyed, many calligraphic masterpieces, particularly formal transcriptions of ancient works commissioned by emperors, were chiseled into stone. A master calligrapher wrote lines from, say, the *Analects* of Confucius on a sheet of paper that was pasted over a polished stone tablet. Meticulous craftsmen lovingly engraved every brushstroke into the stone. Because this process destroyed the original piece of calligraphy, an alternative method was eventually developed: the original masterwork would be traced and the tracing used as a guide for the stone graver's chisel.

Later scholars could reproduce the calligraphy on stone engravings for their private collections by taking rubbings, or "squeezes." A thin sheet of paper was spread across the stone and pressed into every crevice, then rubbed with ink. The characters incised below the surface of the stone showed up white on a black background. Inevitably, an unknown craftsman realized that if he cut the background away from the characters, instead of carving them into the stone's surface, he could produce black writing on white paper. In doing so, he took the short step from rubbing to printing. Of course, printers soon learned that wood was easier to engrave than stone, and used wooden blocks for most of their work. Stone was never abandoned entirely, however, for Chinese bibliophiles have identified books known to have been printed from stone plates.

Because stones themselves can be lost, broken, or simply worn down after centuries of rubbing, remnants of the vast rubbing collections amassed by scholars over the years contribute most to our knowledge of early calligraphic styles. Although rubbings are third-hand reproductions, they are really all we have; old ones are carefully treasured. Books on calligraphy commonly reproduce rubbings as they come off the stone with white characters on a black field.

The calligraphic styles outlined above do not set rigid standards for forming each symbol, as the Western Gothic, Roman, or Uncial scripts do. A medieval friar copying one book of the Gospel in Gothic style formed his letters in exactly the same way as his brother on the next bench. Individuality of writing style was firmly suppressed, only to surface in mischievous marginal decorations.

On the other hand, individuality of style is an estimable feature of Chinese calligraphy. To say that Huizong writes in running style is like saying that Renoir paints in the Impressionist style. That Song emperor's calligraphy is unique, and will always be recognized as his own.

Chinese calligraphy, like Western art, has its calm, orderly classicists and its wild men, its *Fauves*. One calligrapher may be a government official who arises early, meditates, and practices calligraphy before a day full of court responsibilities. Another may be a wandering scholar who does his best work after uncounted bowls of wine. Each master calligrapher's work ought to mirror his personality and life style.

After years of practicing calligraphic styles, our scholar, young no longer, has gained maturity and experience. He is now a master calligrapher, and people gather to watch him at work. What will they see?

Observing a serious calligrapher is rather like watching a Japanese tea ceremony. Both are partly religious, partly aesthetic experiences. For tea master and calligrapher alike, everything must be "just so." The calligrapher prepares by laying out paper precisely where he wants it. Carefully, he sets inkstone and brushes to the left of the paper. He is as fussy about his seating position as a concert pianist before the keyboard.

Patiently, deliberately, the ink is ground, enough for one piece of work. With the grinding goes silent meditation. Onlookers watch, making no sound. When the master has achieved the proper consistency, and when his mind is tranquil, he is ready to take up the brush.

A piece of Chinese calligraphy is, more than any other art, totally spontaneous. No lines are drawn beforehand, no characters are blocked out. The ninefold square was discarded after student years were past. No retracing or patching up is permitted once the brush has traveled its path. That cardinal sin of calligraphy would be humiliatingly obvious to anyone with a modicum of discernment.

Over the centuries, many classically educated students chose to devote their artistic talents to a single-minded pursuit of calligraphy. Many others chose to practice painting and poetry, arts so inextricably twined with calligraphy during all the imperial years of the Middle Kingdom that we will discuss them in this chapter.

From the Tang dynasty onward, painters seemed to belong in opposing studios, either chambers in the imperial palace given over to painters who pleased courtly taste, or bucolic residences inhabited by gentlemen-scholars who painted as a hobby. The first group bowed to established rules of composition, subject matter, and technique, while the second followed an inner creative spirit wherever it led. To gentlemen-scholars, a painting should reveal as much about the artist as the scene he paints: painting for them was like calligraphy, an expression of the whole man.

In both studios, the symbiotic relationship of painting to calligraphy is without equivalent in the West. This relationship begins with medium. In the West, flat, portable pictures from an artist's hand may be executed in oil, watercolor, tempera, acrylic, charcoal, chalk, pencil, or pen and ink. In China, there is just one medium—brush and ink, the same brush and ink used for calligraphy. True, painters may use colored ink as well as black, but it is still the same kind of medium. Court painters often worked on silk for a smooth, elegant effect. Gentlemen-scholars preferred paper for its absorbency, which gave the painting a rough, offhand quality. As time went by, all master painters came to prefer paper.

The West has its letters and its pictures, two entirely different kinds of marks. In China, characters began as pictures, but many have never outgrown their pictographic origins, as we saw in Chapter 2 (Table 2.1). There, painting's most basic purpose, the representation of objects, is also the most basic form of writing, and the technique of painting is rooted in calligraphy as well. Calligraphy is a linear art built of strokes. Chinese paintings are also strongly linear, constructed of calligraphic strokes and imbued with the same life-force thought to vitalize all nature and calligraphy.

One kind of Chinese art more than all the others depends for its quality on the intimate association of painting and calligraphy: bamboo painting. A masterpiece of this genre, so dear to poets and calligraphers, is shown in Figure 7.13. The bamboo, strong and supple, bent but not uprooted by the wind, green all year round, symbolizes the gentleman-scholar. Its graceful stalks and sharply pointed leaves seem to be nature's own handwriting. To capture the appearance and spirit of bamboo in a perfect composition is no mean feat. This exercise in virtuosity has been a standard piece in the repertoire of Chinese art since the period following the breakup of the Han dynasty, and is still taught in traditional Chinese painting classes today.

The bamboo, with its natural calligraphic form, is a perfect foil for the writing we invariably see on a Chinese painting. Until the twentieth century, very few Western painters incorporated writing in their pictures; Chinese painters always have. Traditionally, artists would ask scholar friends to write poetry appropriate to the subject along the side of a painting, or the painter would write a few lines himself. Some hand scrolls are so filled with calligraphy that the painting seems almost secondary. All Chinese painters are competent calligraphers. While a master calligrapher certainly understands the techniques

Fig. 7.13. *Misty Bamboo on a Distant Mountain* by Zheng Xie (1693–1765 A.D.), Qing dynasty. (The Art Museum, Princeton University)

necessary to create a Chinese painting, he may never paint a single picture in his life.

Incidentally, it is easier to create a fake Chinese painting than to forge a calligraphic masterpiece. Often, spurious paintings (and there are many for sale, along with honest copies) are exposed by the forged calligraphy simulating that written on the painting or attached to it by later collectors and commentators.

Another way to judge the authenticity of a painting is to look at the seals that adorn or even deface it. Every educated Chinese possesses a personal seal, often more than one. The archaic characters for his name, or a literary name he chooses, are engraved on small squares or ovals of ivory, wood, marble, glass, bone, or precious metal by highly trained artist-craftsmen still practicing in Hong Kong and overseas Chinese communities.

Seals have been in use since the Shang dynasty. Early seals were used by officials to stamp the clay pressed over cords that bound the covers to wood or bamboo documents. Today's seals are used mostly by private individuals who dip their seals into small containers of semi-solid red ink, then stamp them on silk or paper.

During the European Dark Ages, Daoist priests in China carved Laozi's name into seals and used it to authenticate written charms. Then larger seals were made, encompassing many words, and the ancestor to Chinese printing was born. The Chinese verb *yìn, to leave an impression*, means both *print* and *seal*, and was used for seals that were pressed into clay or dipped in red ink and stamped on paper charms, for wooden blocks carved with pictures or writing, as well as for modern printing presses.

ΕΡ

yìn
(print,
seal)

Today, an artist may stamp his personal seal on his painting, and the scholar who writes poetry along the side will add his seal to identify his contribution. Subsequent owners of the painting will add their seals as well. Many scrolls are enhanced in value because they bear an imperial seal; many others may be defaced by an imperial seal stamped arrogantly across the middle of the painting. In the imperial years, every magistrate had his official seal;

to lose the seal might cause him to lose his office.

Westerners who wish to own a seal may buy one wherever a moderate-sized Chinese community exists. Generally they will be transliterations of the Western surname into ancient Chinese characters.

Calligraphy is the ancestor of painting—an art for the eye—as well as a medium for poetry, an art for both eye and ear. Of Wang Wei, a subject of Tang emperors, it was said, "There is poetry in his painting and painting in his poetry." This statement could apply generally to the arts of poetry and painting in China. Besides being an accomplished scholar, Wang Wei was a calligrapher, painter, and poet, and is ranked as a master of all three. He was not unique; many educated men of his day practiced painting, poetry, and calligraphy.

Certain symbols and images have long been the common property of poets and painters in China. Some of these come from China's treasury of fables and folktales; some are puns, playing on the homonyms so abundant in the Chinese language; some were originated by ancient artists and writers and have now become conventional. The dragon, mentioned in Chapter 4, is a symbol of rain and thunder, rivers and pools. His opposite is the tiger, a traditional representation of courage and strength, associated with fire, wind, and heat. These two opposing forces of nature must be harmoniously balanced before the construction of any building is possible. "Paper tiger" refers to a law not backed by force. A tiger near bamboo pictures the winning combination of courage and endurance.

Other animals significant to painting, the decorative arts, and literature are mandarin ducks, thought to mate for life and so to embody marital fidelity and bliss, and water buffaloes, emblems of coolie labor, overworked but so valued that the law forbade slaughtering them for food. The tortoise, the first creature to live on earth, according to Chinese creation mythology, symbolizes long life, while the fish, whose name in Chinese, *yú*, is a homonym for a word meaning *surplus, excess,* or *leftover,* has come to represent good fortune in a chronically poor country. Likewise, the bat, which you will see decorating Chinese dinnerware, conveys a blessing, for the same spoken word, *fú,* means *happiness* as well as *bat.*

The bamboo, pictured earlier in this chapter, is one symbol of endurance; the pine, which also stays green in winter, is another. Flowers have always been gorgeous subjects for Chinese painters, and the source of countless poetic allusions. The plum blossom, blooming briefly while snow still covers the ground, stands for poetic inspiration and the transience of life; the peony is a metaphor for rank and wealth, the lotus for purity associated with Buddha. The chrysanthemum is loved both in China, where chrysanthemum wine is supposed to lengthen one's life, and in Japan, where it is a symbol of the emperor. Because chrysanthemums bloom in midautumn, they are emblems of the dying year and of the retired bureaucrat writing poetry in his garden.

The writer of poetry in China is never just a poet, or even a painter-poet-calligrapher. To write poetry a person must be educated, of course, and so is certain to have another line of work. He may have passed the civil examinations, aided by a thorough knowledge of poetry, or he may have failed them repeatedly, as did Du Fu (712–770 A.D.), China's greatest poet. For poets succeeding in the imperial examinations there were jobs all over China as magistrates, provincial administrators, courtiers, and librarians. Poets might enter military life, become monks, tend a farm, rule an empire, or chair the Communist party. A few poets were homeless wanderers with no jobs at all and hence no income. One of Du Fu's children died of hunger. And poetry was not reserved entirely for males. The poems of virtuous wives and widows, languishing concubines, and elegant courtesans are still an important part of China's poetic heritage.

Today's Chinese poet writes in a language that has remained virtually unchanged for three thousand years. What does this really mean? Imagine a poet well versed in all European languages reading Theocritus, a Greek poet of the third century B.C.; Beowulf, a seventh-century epic poem written in Old English; Poema del Cid, a twelfth-century Spanish epic; Dante, the thirteenth-century Italian poet; Ronsard, the sixteenth-century French poet; and Donne, the seventeenth-century English poet, as easily as he reads the New York Times, and you have some idea of the length of China's poetic tradition. Chinese poetry reached its peak in the brilliant Tang dynasty, and has declined slowly ever since.

Throughout these long ages, a conflict has always existed in China between those who believed poetry should serve a moral purpose, edifying and instructing its readers, and those who believed poetry was the expression of an individual creative spirit, "art for art's sake." One person could express both points of view. Here is one thing Confucius said about poetry:

Poetry can serve to inspire emotion, to help your observation, to make you fit for company, to express your grievances, to teach you how to serve your father at home and your prince abroad, to enable you to learn the correct names of many birds, beasts, herbs, and trees.*

A few wits looked on poetry only as a technical exercise, a kind of mental gymnastic match for friends who capped rhymes while downing bowls of wine. Today on the Mainland, poetry is definitely not regarded as pure self-expression or as a display of mental agility. The moral philosophy is firmly ascendant, and poems from the past considered "too bourgeois" are strongly suppressed. Poetry must serve the people.

A poet is sure to be influenced by the same feeling for nature that informs art and calligraphy. Good poetry is said to possess that vital breath of life-force, the inspiration of great painting and calligraphy, and Li Bai, China's most famous poet, wrote lines his admirers compared to rushing wind or spring breezes.

From the very beginning, music has been an integral part of Chinese poetry. *The Book of Poetry* is a compilation of lyrics for long lost music. All through China's

---

*James J. Y. Liu, *The Art of Chinese Poetry* (Chicago: University of Chicago Press, 1962), p. 66. © 1962 by James J. Y. Liu. Published 1962. First Phoenix Edition 1966. Third Impression 1970. Printed in the United States of America.

dynasties, new forms of music and new kinds of musical expression created new forms of poetry.

Chinese poets under the emperors were pervasively influenced by wine. To those whose ancestors brewed the strong drinks of northern Europe, Chinese drinking companions seem to hold their liquor poorly. Although some say the Chinese lack an enzyme (alcohol dehydrogenase) that metabolizes ethyl alcohol, the truth is that they often act more drunk than they really are. Chinese poets seem to be in love with the idea of being drunk. The Chinese wine cup does not produce the boisterous drinking songs associated with Western tankards. Wine-inspired poetry may be melancholy or cheerful; lonely or convivial, and always romantic. The degrading aspects of drink are never portrayed.

shī
(poetry)

Chinese poems are generally written in one of two basic forms. The first is *shī*, poems of four-, five-, or seven-syllable lines. Ancient forms of *shī* found in *The Book of Poetry* do not decree a set number of lines, and so allow the poet more freedom than later forms. Usually every other line rhymes. At the beginning of the Tang dynasty, a more structured version of *shī* came into vogue, with a limit of eight five- or seven-syllable lines per poem and a rhyme scheme fixed according to the number of syllables.

詞
cí
(poetry)

Although many *shī* were written for musical accompaniment, poets of the early Song dynasty (960–1279 A.D.) developed a new lyrical form written for contemporary musical themes. This kind of poetry, called *cí*, or *long and short verse*, is often divided into two stanzas with lines of variable length, perhaps one syllable, perhaps eleven. There are over six hundred *cí* forms, each one with a fixed pattern of words and lines named after the original tune, as if "My Country, 'tis of Thee" were still called "God Save the Queen." Unfortunately, the Song musical scores, like those of ancient Zhou, are gone, and their titles, ghosts of lost music like "Dim Fragrance," "Phoenix Hairpin," "Green Jade Cup," "Song of a Dandy," "Bean Leaves Yellow," or "Tipsy in the Flower's Shade," are all that remain.

Chinese poetry in contemporary English translation sounds like the newest kind of modern verse, for translators rarely attempt to reproduce the rhyme scheme. Because Chinese makes so few different sounds available to its speakers, it is an ideal language for rhyming. There are many rhymes, many more than in English, and all Chinese poetry does rhyme. Chinese poetry is shaped by the monosyllabic nature of the Chinese language. When we spoke of the number of syllables per line, we were referring to *zì*, the basic character units of the Chinese language. In a polysyllabic line of English-language poetry like Longfellow's

This is the forest primeval.
The murmuring pines and the hemlocks . . .

stresses on certain syllables create a rhythmic pattern. Not having polysyllabic words to produce a rhythm of stress and non-stress, Chinese poets use different tonal pitches to create variations in sound. Because musical accompaniments are lost, Chinese poetry is no longer sung but often chanted in a way that exaggerates the sing-song quality of the spoken language.

Written prose and everyday spoken Chinese sentences can do very nicely without a subject. So can lines of verse. Chinese poetry frequently eliminates connecting words also, leaving a concise collection of essential words that draw strength and universality from the compact form.

Of all the poets in China — and, as you may have gathered by now, every traditional scholar wrote a poem or two in his lifetime — the most famous in the West is Li Bai. Born in 701 A.D., he grew up in Sichuan, a province known for rich crops and wild, romantic landscapes. (The fantastic-looking mountains seen in Chinese paintings actually exist in Sichuan.) Around the age of twenty, Li Bai left his home, never to settle permanently again, despite four successive wives and several children. His poet friend Du Fu described him as "A waif in the world, his only home is in a cup of wine."*

The youth Li Bai dabbled in knight-errantry, later boasting that he had run his sword through many villainous men. All his life, Li Bai was devoted to the Daoist religion, which by his day had developed a mythology resplendent with immortals gazing from square-pupiled eyes, fairies floating around mountaintops, giant birds swooping through the sky, and white tigers five hundred years old. In the middle of his life, Li Bai called himself

---

*John C. H. Wu, trans., *The Four Seasons of T'ang Poetry* (Rutland, Vermont: Charles E. Tuttle, 1972), p. 58.

a "banished immortal," or, as Westerners might say, a "fallen angel," a spirit exiled from heaven for misdeeds who returns to earth as a superior mortal.

Li Bai, one of those extraordinarily rare Chinese who derived his only income from poetry, never attempted the imperial service examinations and made a great deal of spurning bureaucratic life, of being too busy with drinking and writing poetry to stand for the civil examinations. Yet he did try, repeatedly and unsuccessfully, to obtain a government post through high-placed connections. Several times in his career, he found favor at the emperor's court, even though he was so drunk on one occasion that he had to be doused with water before he could write a piece the emperor wanted immediately. Then, being legendary Li Bai, he dashed off a masterpiece, of course.

Later literary gossips tell us he was banished from court because of slander mouthed by the emperor's favorite eunuch after Li Bai commanded the eunuch to remove his boots, a demeaning service the favorite greatly resented doing. Later in his life, Li Bai was caught between shifting loyalties in a rebellion and thrown into prison for a few months. Although he had no position, no home, and no steady imperial favor, he achieved an enormous reputation as a poet in his own lifetime. He was never destitute, like his friend Du Fu, and in old age traveled on an expensive horse, flanked by servants and singing girls.

Li Bai's love of wine was remarkable even for a country where inspiration from the wine cup is a time-honored literary convention. Legend has it that he drowned after falling out of a boat in a drunken attempt to embrace the moon's reflection. Actually, he died of disease, a fate Western temperance adherents would see as his just deserts, yet the legend truly reflects his image as a romantic rebel who threw away his life in a quest for beauty.

Li Bai wrote many poems in his life; some of them rank among the greatest achievements of world literature. We offer one of them, one that deals with another recurrent theme of Chinese poetry—nostalgia and homesickness. Travel has always been difficult in China because of the rough terrain; even a distance of twenty-five miles represented formidable obstacles to separated friends and families. Government officials had to travel wherever imperial edict sent them; husbands and wives could be parted for years, and children grow up never knowing their fathers.

This poem of Li Bai's is familiar to most Chinese readers, memorized by schoolchildren and quoted by adults. It was written seven centuries before the appearance of a language modern English readers would recognize. The poem is presented first in Chinese characters, with their *Pīnyīn* equivalents and literal English meanings. A more complete English translation follows.

床	*chuáng*	bed
前	*qián*	front
明	*míng*	bright
月	*yuè*	moon
光	*guāng*	light
疑	*yí*	suspect
是	*shì*	to be, is

地	*dì*	land, earth
上	*shàng*	up, above
霜	*shuāng*	frost
舉	*jǔ*	raise
頭	*tóu*	head
望	*wàng*	look
明	*míng*	bright
月	*yuè*	moon
低	*dī*	below, lower
頭	*tòu*	head
思	*sī*	think, consider,
故	*gù*	old, past
鄉	*xiāng*	home, countryside

Brilliant moonlight before my bed
So much like frost-rimed earth.
Bright the moon on my lifted head
That sinks: I think of home.

This poem is an example of verse in the ancient style, which does not precisely define the number of lines in a poem, but limits the number of syllables in each line to five or seven. Rhyme usually occurs at the end of even-numbered lines, the second, fourth, sixth, and so on. In our poem, the end word of the second line, *shuāng*, rhymes with *xiāng*, the last word in the fourth line.

Li Bai wrote these four lines in an extremely simple style, using ordinary words to evoke a vivid picture of a traveler staying at a small, lonely inn, thousands of miles from home. Weary from his day's journey, he cannot drift off to sleep, but lies awake in the moonlit room, falling into a pensive reverie. In this bemused state, he does not immediately recognize the moonlight reflected from the floor, and thinks it frost. Looking up, he sees the moon, and the sight of this familiar light releases a flood of homesickness from his heart.

Like Elizabethan court poets affecting to be shepherds infatuated with simple shepherdesses, the Chinese writer's preoccupation with nostalgia sometimes strikes an artificial note. After all, no one forced Li Bai to traipse thousands of miles from Sichuan. Yet, in the hands of a master, a hackneyed convention can strike the deepest chords of universal emotion. Li Bai is such a master; his poem is particularly poignant today, for in spite of all our sophisticated transportation technology, our railways and highways, our airplanes and ships, hundreds of thousands of Chinese are living far away from their homeland.

Li Bai's poem marks the end of a survey of the Chinese language. We close this book with a final question.

Where does the language go from here?

Its past development is paradoxical. The Chinese language is a highly cultivated refinement of a writing system so primitive it was discarded long ago by Western countries. For all its philosophic and artistic elegance, Chinese is hopelessly clumsy when coping with modern technology. We have seen how inconvenient it is to use a Chinese dictionary or telephone directory, how the Chinese language hampered the development of efficient printing technology, and how awkward Chinese ideographs are for expressing scientific and technological terms. Acronyms like "laser," "DNA," or "AIDS" are impossible in Chinese.

Yet, within this primitive network, the language has evolved into a sophisticated form of communication encompassing the visual beauty of calligraphy on one hand and the intellectual elegance of *wényán* and poetry on the other. We have outlined the decline of *wényán*. As time goes by, only a handful of scholars will study the literary language intensively enough to master it.

Simplifying a character from fifteen to five strokes certainly takes the essence of pleasurable accomplishment out of calligraphy. With the increasing dependence on word processors based on *Pīnyīn* Romanization, it is not inconceivable that in another generation or two most people will be unable to write Chinese characters.

These changes are inevitable, it seems, if China is to catch up industrially with the West and prevent the kind of debasement it suffered at the end of the nineteenth century from happening again. But quick advances extract an enormous price. Ironically, the linguistic achievements of several thousand years have finally proved to be too great a burden for a people caught between old culture and new technology. In their eagerness to cast off such a burden and move toward a more efficient means of expression, the Chinese may throw away a treasure that can never be regained.

Appendix I

CHRONOLOGICAL CHART OF CHINESE DYNASTIES

Xia	ca. 2205–ca. 1766 B.C.
Shang	ca. 1766–ca. 1122 B.C.
Zhou	ca. 1122–249 B.C.
Qin	221–207 B.C.
Han	202 B.C.–220 A.D.
Three Kingdoms	220–264
Jin	265–420
Southern and Northern Dynasties	386–581
Sui	589–617
Tang	618–906
Five Dynasties	907–960

Song	960–1279
Yuan	1279–1368
Ming	1368–1644
Qing	1644–1912
Republic	1912–
People's Republic	1949–

3000	2500	2000	1500	1000	500
NEOLITHIC		XIA	SHANG	ZHOU	CH'IN · HAN

Huang-ti "Yellow Emperor"

Animals domesticated

Bronze Age

Iron Age   Warring states

Settlement in Yellow River basin

Wheat and millet cultivated

Ancestor worship

Oracle bones

Confucius

Laozi   Shihuangdi

Sericulture

Early writing

Sophisticated written language

Book of Poetry   Great Wall

I Ching

Flood control

Sun spots observed

Painted pottery

Potter's wheel

Bronze vessels

Jade and ivory carving begins

Crossbow

Traction plow

Pictograph

Brush and ink first used

Black pottery

Large seal script   Small seal script

Feudalism

Buddha (India)

← — EGYPTIANS — →

← — GREEKS — →

← — MINOANS — →

← ROMANS —

← — SUMERIANS — → ← — BABYLONIANS — →

Cuneiform script

Phoenician culture flowers

Julius Caesar

Hieroglyphics

Latin language appears

Cheops' Great Pyramid

Hammurabi

Abraham   Tutankhamen

Golden Age of Athens

Stonehenge

Moses

Alexander the Great

Trojan War

Aristotle

Meton   Classical Latin

Kings David and Solomon

Fall of Jerusalem

500   **1000**

HAN	PERIOD OF DISUNITY	SUI	TANG	SONG	YUAN	MING

Buddhism introduced

Compass

Imperial university and library

Paper invented

Alchemy

Wall painting

Regular, running, cursive styles

Wang Xizhi

Tea

Kite

Birth of landscape painting

Buddhist sculpture and architecture

Bamboo painting begins

"Life-force" defined in art criticism

Grand Canal started

Civil-service examination begins

Li Bai

Du Fu

Golden Age of poetry

Zen Buddhism spreads

Empress Wu

Emperor Li

Wang Wei

Porcelain perfected

Foot binding

Block printing

Emperor Huizong

Cí poetry

Vernacular tales

Gunpowder

Paper currency

Movable type

Classic age of painting and ceramics

Mongol rule

Genghis Khan

Kublai Khan

Musical drama

Bamboo and horse painting

Three Kingdoms

Water Margin

ROMAN EMPIRE MIDDLE AGES RENAISSANCE

Jesus Christ ———————————➤

Marcus Aurelius

Catholic Church

Monasteries centers of culture

Germans conquer Roman Empire

Attila the Hun

Vulgar Latin

German appears

Saxons conquer England

◄——————— MAYANS ———————

Pope Gregory and primacy of Roman Pope

Charle-magne

Old English

Romance language appears

Beowulf

Book of Kells

Spanish and Italian appear ➤

Crusades

VIKINGS

Magna Carta

Chaucer

Marco Polo

Giotto

Battle of Hastings

◄——— Feudalism ———➤

Dante

Middle English

Poema de Cid

Incas

MING	QING	

Beijing capital	Manchus rule	Sun Yat-sen
Jesuits and Portuguese traders	Queue imposed	Chiang Kai-shek
		Hu Shih
	Emigration from Guangdong and Fujian	Overthrow of imperial government
	Opium War	Japanese occupation
	Dream of the Red Chamber	Mao Zedong
		Zhou En-lai
		Emancipation of women
Collectors and connoisseurs in art		Qi Bai-shi
		Zhang Da-qian

RENAISSANCE

	Reformation	Locke	Queen Victoria
	Martin Luther	Newton	Freud
Gutenberg Bible	Cervantes	American Revolution	First and Second World Wars
	Shakespeare		Hitler
Modern English	Galileo	Mozart	F. D. Roosevelt
Columbus	Gregorian calendar	Beethoven	
da Vinci	Donne	Napoleon	Einstein
Michelangelo		U.S. Civil War	
Copernicus		Schliemann	
Henry VIII			
Ronsard		Marx	

SOME COMMON RADICALS

Number of Strokes	Radical	Pīnyīn	Meaning	Example
One	`			丸 (pill)
	丨			上 (up)
	丿			九 (nine)
	乙	yǐ	Second of the 10 "heavenly stems"	沘 (pond)
	一	yī	one	下 (down)
Two	亠		a cover	夜 (night)

Number of Strokes	Radical	Pīnyīn	Meaning	Example	
	冫		ice	冷	(winter)
	冖		a cover	冠	(hat)
	几	jī	end table	凳	(stool)
	凵		receptacle	函	(a box)
	刀	dāo	knife	分	(divide)
	力	lì	strength	男	(male)
	勹		wrap	包	(include)
	匚		box	匠	(craftsman)
	卜	bǔ	divine	卦	(diagram)
	卩		seal	印	(print)
	阝		left ear	防	(protect)
	阝		right ear	郁	(flourishing)
	十	shí	ten	古	(ancient)
	二	èr	two	井	(well)
	人	rén	person	他	(he)
	又	yòu	again	双	(a pair)
Three	宀		roof	家	(home)
	广		shelter	床	(bed)
	氵		water	河	(river)
	口	kǒu	mouth	吃	(eat)
	囗		enclosure	囚	(prisoner)
	山	shān	mountain	屹	(rise high)
	工	gōng	work	功	(merit)
	土	tú	soil	地	(land)
	士	shì	scholar	志	(purpose)

Number of Strokes	Radical	Pīnyīn	Meaning	Example
	女	nǔ	female	她 (she)
	小	xiǎo	small	少 (scarce)
	大	dà	large	夫 (husband)
	子	zǐ	son	孩 (child)
	尸	shī	corpse	尾 (tail)
	卝		grass top	花 (flower)
	忄		heart	性 (character)
	彡		feathery	杉 (fir wood)
	犭		mammal	猫 (cat)
	弓	gōng	bow	躬 (to bow)
	彳		walk	行 (to walk)
	巛		stream	災 (calamity)
	夕	xī	evening	汐 (night tides)
	幺	yāo	tiny	幼 (young)
	巾	jīn	towel	布 (cloth)
Four	毛	máo	hair	毡 (felt)
	手	shǒu	hand	拜 (to greet)
	日	rì	sun	明 (bright)
	月	yuè	moon	朋 (friends)
	曰	yuē	speak	書 (books)
	木	mù	wood	林 (forest)
	水	shuǐ	water	冰 (ice)
	火	huǒ	fire	焚 (burn)
	心	xīn	heart	念 (think of)
	父	fù	father	爺 (grandfather)

Number of Strokes	Radical	Pīnyīn	Meaning	Example	
	王	wáng	king	玉	(jade)
	牛	niú	ox	牲	(livestock)
	户	hù	family	房	(house)
	戈	gē	spear	战	(battle)
	气	qì	gas	氧	(oxygen)
	欠	qiàn	to owe	歉	(apology)
	爿	pán	a piece of wood	牀	(bed)
	犬	quǎn	dog	獸	(animal)
	斤	jīn	ax	斥	(rebuke)
	歹	dǎi	bad	殘	(cruel)
Five	石	shí	stone	碇	(stone anchor)
	目	mù	eyes	盲	(blind)
	四		flat eye	買	(to buy)
	田	tián	field	男	(male)
	皿	mǐu	vessel	盆	(tub)
	穴	xué	cave	窄	(narrow)
	立	lì	to stand	妾	(concubine)
	疒		disease	疗	(to cure)
	衤		clothes	袖	(sleeves)
	用	yòng	use	甩	(throw away)
	矢	shí	arrow	知	(to know)
	白	bái	white	皇	(emperer)
	皮	pí	skin	皺	(wrinkles)

Number of Strokes	Radical	Pīnyīn	Meaning	Example
Six	禾	hé	grain	季 (season)
	母	mǔ	mother	每 (every)
	自	zì	self	息 (rest)
	舟	zhōu	boat	航 (travel)
	米	mǐ	rice	粥 (rice porridge)
Seven	耳	ěr	ear	取 (to take)
	衣	yī	clothes	裝 (apparel)
	羽	yǔ	feathers	翁 (old man)
	竹	zhú	bamboo	竿 (pole)
	虫	chóng	insects	蚊 (mosquito)
	老	lǎo	old	耄 (80–90 years old)
	舌	shé	tongue	甜 (sweet)
	西	xī	west	要 (to want)
	頁	yè	page	順 (agreeable)
	言	yán	speech	誓 (to swear)
	豆	dòu	beans	頭 (head)
	車	chē	vehicle	輪 (wheel)
	足	zú	foot	跑 (to run)
	身	shēn	body	躬 (to bow)
	角	jiǎo	horn	觔 (tendons)
	辛	xīn	bitter	辣 (hot)
	見	guān	look	覘 (to spy)
	豸	zhì	worm	貓 (cat)

Number of Strokes	Radical	*Pīnyīn*	Meaning	Example	
	里	lǐ	Chinese mile	重	(heavy)
Eight	雨	yǔ	rain	雷	(thunder)
	金	jīn	gold	銅	(copper)
	門	mén	door	閂	(latch of a door)
	其	qí	it, he	基	(foundation)
	青	qīng	green	靜	(quiet)
Nine	骨	gú	bone	骷	(skeleton)
	革	gé	leather	鞋	(shoe)
	風	fēng	wind	颱	(typhoon)
Ten	馬	mǎ	horse	騎	(to ride)
	鬥	dòu	struggle	鬧	(be noisy)
	鬼	guǐ	ghost	魅	(demon)
Eleven	魚	yú	fish	魴	(a bream)
	鳥	niǎo	bird	鴨	(duck)
	麻	mā	hemp	摩	(to touch)
Twelve	黑	hēi	black	墨	(Chinese ink stick)
	龍	lóng	dragon	聾	(deaf)

Appendix 3

BIRTH YEARS AND CHARACTERISTICS OF THE TWELVE ANIMAL SIGNS

Year of the Rat (鼠): 1900, 1912, 1924, 1936, 1948, 1960, 1972, 1984, 1996, 2008, 2020

Your determination to be the best in all you do makes you a hard-working perfectionist at work and play, and, incidentally, a fine dancer. Your assets are thrift, honesty, and control over your emotions, but a love of gossip may undo you.

Year of the Ox (牛): 1901, 1913, 1925, 1937, 1949, 1961, 1973, 1985, 1997, 2009, 2021

Your calmness, patience, and superior speaking ability make you an excellent parent or teacher. In sports like tennis, a quick mind and quick tongue are your most formidable assets. You are manually dexterous and inclined to be stubborn.

Year of the Tiger (虎): 1902, 1914, 1926, 1938, 1950, 1962, 1974, 1986, 1998, 2010, 2022

You are strong, fearless, and impetuous. To your friends you are sensitive, thoughtful, and sympathetic, but you have little respect for those in authority and find it hard to curb a short temper.

Year of the Rabbit (兔): 1903, 1915, 1927, 1939, 1951, 1963, 1975, 1987, 1999, 2011, 2023

You are lucky, clever, and generally talented, as well as reserved and conservative. Although you are kind and loving, your closest family finds you distant. You could do well in business and probably will have a tranquil life.

Year of the Dragon (龍): 1904, 1916, 1928, 1940, 1952, 1964, 1976, 1988, 2000, 2012, 2024

You have energy, good health, animal magnetism, and an ability to inspire trust and confidence, but your strong tendency to eccentricity, your stubbornness, and quick temper may cause trouble. You are thrifty and need plenty of affection; you marry early or not at all.

Year of the Snake (蛇): 1905, 1917, 1929, 1941, 1953, 1965, 1977, 1989, 2001, 2013, 2025

You will never want for money. Handsome and passionate, you attract a mate, but may not remain faithful. Your intensity and general distrust of other people (especially those born in the Year of the Snake) make communication difficult. You rarely ask for advice.

Year of the Horse (馬): 1906, 1918, 1930, 1942, 1954, 1966, 1978, 1990, 2002, 2014, 2026

You are everybody's friend because of your self-confidence, skill, cheerful loquacity, perceptivity, and good looks. Your hot temper may cause you to lose the respect of others. You manage money well. Your love of freedom makes you leave home early.

Year of the Sheep (羊): 1907, 1919, 1931, 1943, 1955, 1967, 1979, 1991, 2003, 2015, 2027

You are known for an artistic good taste, a sense of style, and a tranquil disposition that makes you a good marriage partner. You never have money problems. You are also shy, and you have a pessimistic, quizzical view of life. You can be easily duped by people who play on your sympathies.

Year of the Monkey (猴): 1908, 1920, 1932, 1932, 1944, 1956, 1968, 1980, 1992, 2004, 2016, 2028

You are quick-moving, quick-thinking, quarrelsome, mercurial, and crafty. You think little of others, yet enjoy hearing good things about yourself. Because you can easily solve intricate problems, including those involving money, you usually succeed on the job, although you cannot maintain a sustained interest in any project.

Year of the Cock (雞): 1909, 1921, 1933, 1945, 1957, 1969, 1981, 1993, 2005, 2017, 2029

Your loyalty, hard work, honesty, and trustworthiness make you a good leader. You fight tenaciously for a just cause. Though you will never be wealthy, you will always be comfortably well off. You are emotionally distant from others, obstinate, and prone to scolding.

Year of the Dog (狗): 1910, 1922, 1934, 1946, 1958, 1970, 1982,
1994, 2006, 2018, 2030

You are a capable, skilled worker, loyal to your boss. Also, you are
strongly self-centered, opinionated, and subject to radical swings
in emotion. Anger so overcomes you that you sometimes take fool-
ish chances. Many projects you begin never get finished.

Year of the Pig (猪): 1911, 1923, 1935, 1947, 1959, 1971, 1983,
1995, 2007, 2019, 2031

Affectionate and kindhearted, you focus all your considerable
knowledge and skill on tasks that come your way. You hate to
quarrel. Money slips through your fingers, and you must fight a
tendency to be lazy.

BIBLIOGRAPHY

Listed below are books for readers who want to know more about China and the Chinese language as it relates to art and literature. Most were chosen for their interest and readability. Unfortunately, some are out of print, but well worth a trip to the library.

Blunden, Caroline, and Mark Elvin. *Cultural Atlas of China.* Rev. ed. New York: Checkmark Books, 1998.
　　Maps, tables, photographs, and art enrich this focused survey of China's history and culture.
Carter, Thomas Francis. *The Invention of Printing in China and Its Spread Westward.* 2d ed. Revised by L. Carrington Goodrich. New York: Ronald Press, 1955.
　　Even someone with no interest in Chinese printing will be drawn to this pioneering piece of scholarship by its lively, readable style.
Chiang Yee. *Chinese Calligraphy: An Introduction to Its Aesthetic and Technique.* 3d ed., rev. Cambridge, Mass.: Harvard University Press, 1973.

Introduces the art to Westerners and illuminates the "soul" of Chinese calligraphy as well.

Driscoll, Lucy, and Kenji Toda. *Chinese Calligraphy.* 2d ed. New York: Paragon Book Reprint Corp., 1964.

Gathers the thoughts of Chinese writers on calligraphy over the ages. Illustrated with rubbings.

Fong, Wen C. *Beyond Representation: Chinese Painting and Calligraphy, 8th to 14th Century.* New Haven, Conn.: Yale University Press, 1992.

A lavishly illustrated history of Chinese art, distinguished by high quality reproductions.

Fu, Shen C. Y., Marilyn W. Fu, Mary G. Neill, and Mary Jane Clark. *Traces of the Brush: Studies in Chinese Calligraphy.* New Haven, Conn.: Yale University Art Gallery, 1977.

Contains essays on various aspects of Chinese calligraphy.

Ho, Minfong, translator. *Maples in the Mist.* Illustrated by Jean and Mou-sien Tseng. New York: Lothrop, Lee & Shepard, 1996.

The most beloved poems from the Tang Dynasty, written in English and Chinese, collected in a children's picture book that recalls the combination of painting and poetry found on Chinese scrolls. A book for all ages.

Hucker, Charles O. *China's Imperial Past; an Introduction to Chinese History and Culture.* Stanford, Cal.: Stanford University Press, 1975.

A well-organized survey of China's long history.

Liu, James J. Y. *The Art of Chinese Poetry.* Chicago, Ill.: University of Chicago Press, 1962.

Describes the technical and thematic aspects of Chinese poetry for a reader with some background in literary criticism.

Liu, Wu-chi, and Irving Yucheng Lo, eds. *Sunflower Splendor: Three Thousand Years of Chinese Poetry.* Bloomington: Indiana University Press, 1990.

Every era in China's long poetic tradition is represented in this comprehensive collection of poetry. The poems were translated directly from Chinese by over fifty contributors.

Paludan, Ann. *Chronicle of the Chinese Emperors; the Reign-by-Reign Record of the Rulers of Imperial China.* London: Thames & Hudson, 1998.

Abundantly illustrated with works of Chinese art, this very useful reference book summarizes the highlights of Chinese history.

Spence, Jonathan. *The Search for Modern China.* New York: W. W. Norton, 1990.
  A scholarly account of China's history from the seventeenth to twentieth century.
Sullivan, Michael. *The Arts of China.* 4th ed. Berkeley: University of California Press, 1999.
  A complete introduction to Chinese art from the Stone Age to the present.
Temple, Robert. *The Genius of China; 3000 Years of Science, Discovery, and Invention.* Introduction by Joseph Needham. New York: Simon & Schuster, 1986.
  A summary of the Joseph Needham's lifetime research into the history of Chinese science, handsomely illustrated.
Weiger, L. *Chinese Characters: Their Origin, Etymology, History, Classification, and Signification.* 2d ed., rev. Translated by L. Davrout. New York: Paragon Book Reprint Corp., 1965.
  Originally published in 1927, this foray into Chinese etymology will be useful mainly to advanced students of Chinese.
Yang Xiaoneng, editor. *The Golden Age of Chinese Archaeology; Celebrated Discoveries from the People's Republic of China.* New Haven, Conn.: Yale University Press, 1999.
  A catalog of an exhibition of remarkable antiquities from prehistoric times to the tenth century that toured Washington, Houston, and San Francisco in 2000.
Yang Xin, and others. *Three Thousand Years of Chinese Painting.* New Haven, Conn.: Yale University Press, 1997.
  A comprehensive, richly illustrated survey that includes modern Chinese art.